Kerry V. Kern

Labrador Retrievers

Second Edition

Everything about Purchase, Care, Nutrition,
Diseases, Breeding, and Behavior

With 52 Color Photographs
Illustrations by Michele Earle-Bridges

Consulting Editor: Matthew M. Vriends, Ph.D.

BARRON'S

About the author
Kerry Kern, who has written extensively on canine topics, is the author of Barron's *Siberian Huskies* and *The New Terrier Handbook.*

All inquiries should be addressed to:
Barron's Educational Series, Inc.
250 Wireless Boulevard
Hauppauge, NY 11788

International Standard Book No. 0-8120-9018-7

Library of Congress Catalog Card No. 94-46722

Library of Congress Cataloging-in-Publication Data

Kern, Kerry V.
    Labrador retrievers: everything about purchase, care, nutrition, breeding, behavior, and training / Kerry V. Kern: with color photographs by well-known photographers and drawings by Michele Earle-Bridges.
        p. cm.
    Includes bibliographical references (p.) and index.
    ISBN 0-8120-9018-7
    1. Labrador retriever. I. Earle-Bridges, Michele. II. Title.
SF429.L3K47 1995   94-46722
636.7'52—dc20   CIP

Printed in Hong Kong

5678   9955   987654321

Photo credits
Barbara Augello: front cover, inside front cover, pages 86, 87, back cover; Eugene Butenas (LCA Photogaphy): pages 13 (top), 42 (top), 70 (top); Michele Earle-Bridges: pages 43 (bottom), 90; Susan Green: pages 16, 17, 30–31, 35, 76, 82; D.J. Hamer: 42 (bottom), 59: Lillian Knoblock (Highland Kennels): pages 12, 91 (top left, bottom); James Pitrone (The Seeing Eye): page 55; Lorraine Robbenharr: pages 39 (Ch. Kupros Spartacus), 62 (bottom); Judith Strom: pages 9, 21, 27, 51, 58, 67, 70 (bottom), 91 (top right), inside back cover; William van Vught: pages 4, 8, 13 (bottom), 43 (top), 62 (top), 63, 73.

Important Note
    This pet owner's guide tells the reader how to buy and care for a Labrador retriever. The author and the publisher consider it important to point out that the advice given in the book is meant primarily for normally developed puppies from a good breeder—that is, dogs of excellent physical health and good character.
    Anyone who adopts a fully grown dog should be aware that the animal has already formed its basic impressions of human beings. The new owner should watch the animal carefully, including its behavior toward humans, and should meet the previous owner. If the dog comes from a shelter, it may be possible to get some information on the dog's background and peculiarities there. There are dogs that as a result of bad experiences with humans behave in an unnatural manner or may even bite. Only people who have experience with dogs should take in such an animal.
    Even well-behaved and carefully supervised dogs sometimes do damage to someone else's property or cause accidents. It is therefore in the owner's interest to be adequately insured against such eventualities, and we strongly urge all dog owners to purchase a liability policy that covers their dog.

Contents

Preface

Labrador retrievers have come a long way in a relatively short time. Only a few Labradors had been imported to the United States in the early part of this century; today the breed ranks among the top five for the number of litters registered each year with the American Kennel Club, accounting for many thousands of new dogs annually. Such skyrocketing popularity often hurts much more than it helps a breed in terms of overall quality. Because Labrador retrievers are such well-rounded dogs, popular not only as house pets but also as hunting, working, and show dogs, the breed has so far escaped most of the indiscriminate mass breedings that often result from too much notoriety. Field and hunting enthusiasts have made it their job to breed the best sporting dogs possible, and this endeavor requires a dog with good structure. Show and obedience competitors have not only maintained but enhanced the quality of show and breeding stock. They should be commended.

Today, Labrador retrievers are in great demand, and rightfully so because they are terrific dogs. However, among pet stock are not only fine quality animals, but lesser specimens as well. It is my fervent hope that everyone who reads this book and owns a Labrador will safeguard this wonderful breed by loving and taking good care of his or her pet, and by attempting to breed only superior dogs from superior backgrounds. In this way the Labrador retriever will hopefully escape the physical decline other breeds have suffered and exhibited in unsound temperaments, poor structure, and debilitating diseases. Most Labradors have so far been spared this fate, but the danger is mounting with every haphazard mating.

The material presented in this book covers the practical aspects of owning and caring for a Labrador retriever, as well as a brief look into the breed's history and heritage as a worker for man. As a general introduction to the breed, it is not intended to delve into health topics best left to a veterinarian, but instead to focus on the particulars of this breed and what a good owner must do to form the man-dog bond that is at the heart of a good relationship. Step-by-step instructions on how to teach the basic commands are provided.

I would like to acknowledge the help of Helen Warwick, a noted breeder, judge, and writer, who aided me in obtaining much of the historical information contained in this book. She died during the writing of the original manuscript and is sorely missed. Pat Donnelly was also of great help, as were numerous breeders who eagerly shared their opinions and expertise in a desire to see their breed presented in the best, most accurate way. Thanks, also, to Helgard Niewisch, D.V.M., for reviewing the manuscript, to Matthew Vriends, Ph.D., and to Fredric L. Frye, D.V.M., for many suggestions incorporated in this new edition.

This book is dedicated to those who dedicate their life's work to our hardy, intelligent Labrador retriever.

Kerry V. Kern
January 1995

Considerations Before You Buy

Is a Labrador Retriever the Right Dog for you?

Before you start canvassing local dealers and breeders, take the time to evaluate your lifestyle and the suitability of a dog, specifically a Labrador, in your home. If you answer "yes" to a few key questions, the selection process can begin:

• *Is there a place in my life for a dog?* A good owner must commit to training the dog thoroughly in the basic commands and supplying it with daily love, attention, adequate housing, and an outlet for its energy. Although not an overly large or high-strung dog, the Labrador retriever does need ample space and some regular exercise. Owners must make a lifelong commitment, meaning daily walks for approximately the next ten years.

• *Does everyone in the household agree to acquiring a puppy?* Despite good intentions, owners sometimes find other family members who did not want a dog around suddenly becoming "allergic" to it or finding it a nuisance. Such situations generally spell disaster for the dog, so think carefully and discuss this acquisition with all involved.

• *Do I really want a puppy* ? Puppies require much attention and training while young. They will need frequent walks and access to the outside during the housebreaking process. An older dog may be more appropriate for those who cannot be at home during long stretches of time.

• *Can I afford a Labrador retriever?* Aside from the initial purchase price, an owner must supply routine veterinary care and an adequate, nutritious diet. Such costs are considerable and constant throughout the dog's life.

Selecting Your Labrador

Once you have resolved that the Labrador retriever really is the dog for you, you must decide what type you are looking for in order to find the best source for your dog. Are you looking for a companion, for a gun dog, or for a field or show competitor? If you are looking for a pet, your resources are many. If you are searching for a potential winner in competitive contests, you need to do some research and make a careful selection.

Hunting dogs: With hunting companions, your best bet is to locate an established shooting kennel with active working stock. A Labrador retriever bred from such lines should naturally have very keen retrieving instincts and desires. The puppies will probably already have been exposed to the sound of gunfire, and any animal exhibiting gun-shyness will have been noted as an unlikely hunting dog and made available to a more suitable home. A gun dog should appear vital, bold, and in good trim, even as a puppy. At eight weeks of age, it should eagerly chase after and attempt to pick up a stick or ball thrown near it, but passing this little test only indicates that the natural instincts are present. It certainly is not a reliable indicator of later ability.

Field trial dogs: If you are looking for a field-trial competitor, you should seek the advice of breeders who actively compete or have produced winners in the past. There is no magic formula for spotting a future national champion. Experienced breeders can make an educated prediction based on the pedigree behind the dog and their evaluation of the puppy in its early stages. But producing a field-trial competitor is a two-way street: a competent worker is needed to begin with, but the owner must be able to instruct efficiently and nurture the dog to attain its potential.

Show dogs: Selecting a puppy destined to be a show dog is even more of a gamble, especially since most puppies are purchased while eight to ten weeks of age—a time of rapid development when little of the mature physique can be accurately predicted. The Labrador retriever develops rather slowly, reaching physical maturity at 18 to 24 months. Selections made prior to this are at best guesses, and should therefore be based upon pedigree and the breeder's knowledge of his or her dogs. If possible, hold off purchasing a show prospect until it is four to six months of age, when a slightly more reliable evaluation can be made. Puppies deemed "show quality" generally demand a hefty purchase price.

Companion dogs: Those fanciers seeking a companion have many outlets. The breeders mentioned above should also be able to supply "pet-quality" dogs—well-bred, quality Labradors that have been eliminated from competitive status for some minor fault that makes them unsuitable for the show ring or stakes competition. Such puppies are often very safe bets, as the pedigrees of both dam and sire are known and the puppies have been raised during the formative stages of life by knowledgeable people. The price of such puppies, reflecting the heritage behind them and the care they have been given, will generally range from several hundred dollars up.

Pet Labradors can also be purchased from pet stores or neighborhood litters. If you consider a pet-store dog, I suggest that you investigate from where the puppy was purchased and get as much information as possible on its initial care. Many pet shops have been branded—often without foundation—as selling inferior, often unhealthy puppies purchased from the "puppy mills" of midwestern America where the animals are mass-produced from whatever breeding stock is at hand. However, small local kennels often supply respectable pet stores, too; research should quickly tell you about the pet-store puppy's beginnings. Labradors bought from pet shops are often priced the same as pet-quality dogs available at established kennels.

As for neighborhood litters, this is as popular a source as any for quality pets at a reasonable price. I would recommend that you verify that both the mother and father are registered purebreds before you buy, and that your puppy's litter is registered or eligible for registration with the American Kennel Club. Without such confirmation you cannot be assured that you are buying a purebred Labrador, and the price should reflect this.

To help in your search, the names and addresses of local field-trial clubs, show clubs, and national Labrador retriever organizations can be obtained by writing to the American Kennel Club, 51 Madison Avenue, New York, New York 10010. Another informative source is the AKC's publication, *Purebred Dogs: American Kennel Gazette*. It is issued monthly and contains a breed column, a list of advertising kennels, information on all aspects of dog care, and upcoming show and trial listings.

What to Look for in a Labrador Puppy

Regardless of how you intend to use your Labrador retriever puppy, it

Side by side, puppies may look the same, but you should examine each dog carefully to evaluate its physical traits and behavior.

should be carefully evaluated for general health and essential breed characteristics. Before you inspect your potential pet, take a close look at the environment it has been raised in. The kennel or living quarters should be neat, clean, and free from parasites. Try to see the litter as a whole. Attempting to choose a good puppy from a poor litter is at best risky.

It is preferable that you see both dam (female parent) and sire (male parent), as this should give you a general impression of the size and type of stock from which your litter stems. In many cases only the dam is available, but even she should indicate whether the litter traces to healthy beginnings. Remember, however, that the dam may appear run-down due to the rigors of whelping and nursing a litter. If this is the case, ask to see a prepregnancy picture. If your puppy's litter is the result of a repeat mating, ask to see some of the maturing dogs from the previous lit-

ter or for the name and phone number of an owner. This is especially important when purchasing a show prospect.

In evaluating an eight-week-old puppy, look first at its overall appearance. Remember that most of the dog's growth will take place during the first 12 months and that different skeletal areas grow at different rates. A dog at this early stage is apt to appear slightly out of balance. However, a puppy should be clean, pleasant smelling, and plump (but not bloated, which can indicate a worm infestation). The eyes should be clear and without discharge and the ears should appear pink inside.

The outline of the dog should appear strong, with a short back and heavy-boned legs. The puppy should be full of enthusiasm and not shy away too easily. To test this, remove it from its littermates and see if it still continues to wag its tail or show interest in play. Timidity is not typical of a Labrador retriever.

Important breed characteristics are the otter tail (see page 68); the short, dense, hard-feeling coat; and the warm, kindly expression. A slight variation in size among littermates is normal, and the largest puppy should not be deemed most desirable simply on this account.

If you are buying for show, you will naturally concentrate on the physical attributes. If you are buying for the field, you must look deeper to the invisible qualities. Put the puppy to two simple tests. Focus on its retrieving instincts by sitting next to the puppy while it is alone. Make sure you have its attention, then throw a small toy or crumpled piece of paper several feet in front of it. Verbally encourage the pup to get it. A likely candidate will want to pick up the object almost immediately. A puppy that sees the throw but ignores it may be disinterested in retrieving. To evaluate a puppy's potential response to training, place the puppy on the ground or floor and stand five feet away from it. Bend and call it to you. A good candidate will move toward you immediately, appearing pleased to be involved. Such an animal is eager to please and comfortable around humans—necessary qualities in a dog expected to endure the rigors of field training.

These rudimentary tests are by no means the last word on puppy evaluation. They are simply indicators of potential.

What Age Is Best?

Most puppies are purchased at eight to 10 weeks of age, when they are developmentally in what is known as the "human socialization period." This period, which only lasts until the puppy is about 12 weeks of age, is the best time in a dog's life for it to learn to live with humans.

It is recommended that a puppy be separated from its dam and littermates and placed in the home during the eighth week of life because it is forming permanent bonds at this time. If allowed to remain with the litter, the primary bond will be to dogs rather than humans, which is a hindrance to the human-dog relationship.

Conversely, it is also important that removal from the litter does not occur *before* eight weeks—during the "canine socialization period"—because this period with dam and littermates is essential to produce a dog that can get along with other animals. If removed too early, the puppy may not have fully learned the lessons of animal socialization and the end result is likely to be an adult dog that reacts overly aggressively or submissively whenever it meets another dog. Such dogs often

become fighters or "fear biters" who are so easily upset that they lash out at other dogs and people.

Pet-shop puppies are sometimes taken from their litters at six or seven weeks of age so that they can arrive in the stores at the most "adorable" age— eight weeks. While this gets the puppies to the market at their most "saleable" time, it can have dire effects on the normal socialization process.

My Tip: If you cannot arrange to pick up your puppy at approximately eight or nine weeks of age, be sure it is being raised with humans rather than left with the litter until you can bring it home.

There is no more loving companion than a Labrador puppy. Given lots of attention, a young Lab will grow up well socialized and content with its position in the family.

The Purchase Agreement

Once you have selected your puppy and settled with the breeder on a purchase price, make it official by putting the terms of the deal in writing. This often saves later difficulty should the dog prove unacceptable for health reasons or should you fail to receive all the documents promised you. It is routine for the breeder to allow the new owner a set number of days to return the puppy should it fail a health examination by the new owner's veterinarian. Get this in writing. The terms of such an agreement should also clarify whether an ill dog will be replaced with another or if the purchase price will be refunded.

At the time of the sale, the breeder should supply you with the puppy's American Kennel Club registration application, most of which is filled out by the breeder. This application includes the names and AKC numbers of the sire and dam, information on the litter from which the puppy was whelped, and the name and address of the person to whom the ownership of the puppy is being transferred. The new owner completes the form by listing two possible names for the puppy, signing, and enclosing the proper fee. If all is in order, the paperwork should take about three to four weeks to process. If the breeder has been following proper procedure (and be wary of those who have not), he or she should have registered the puppy's litter with the AKC at birth and received these applications prior to the sale. Should the applications not be available, be sure to get a signed bill of sale from the breeder stating the breed, sex, and color of the puppy; the date of birth; and the registered names of the sire and dam, with numbers, if available. This information is vital should you need to contact the American Kennel Club in search of "missing" papers.

If you are buying a puppy from a show-oriented kennel, you may find that the breeder has some additional terms you must deal with. In the case of a top-quality animal, the breeder may stipulate terms concerning the future mating of the dog. (But, quite honestly, in most cases a breeder would not let go of what he or she feels is a potential top contender in the first place.) With pet-quality puppies from such kennels the breeder may only agree to sell the dog upon agreement that it not be bred. In the case of a puppy carrying a disqualifying fault, the breeder may even withhold the puppy's registration papers until proof is supplied that the dog has been neutered. In return, the breeder may offer an attractive selling price to close such a deal. In this way the breeder is trying to eliminate faulty, genetically inferior animals from passing along their faults to future generations. Such dogs will still make fine pets. If you cannot abide by such arrangements, look elsewhere.

Basic Rules of Labrador Care

The day-to-day care you give your Labrador retriever reflects your commitment to pet ownership. On the whole, Labrador retrievers are not burdens to own. They require little grooming, are generally very hardy, learn manners fairly easily, and don't need (or want) to run a marathon daily to stay in shape. Being easygoing doesn't mean they can be neglected, however. It is the owner's responsibility to tend to all the basic needs.

Socialization

If you are a novice in dog ownership, you and your puppy may greatly benefit from attending a puppy socialization class. Such classes are sponsored by local breed or obedience clubs for owners of eight- to twenty-two-week-old puppies. The object of such classes is not only to teach puppies simple positive behaviors (walk on lead, sit, come) in a nonstressful manner, but also to help owners become good masters. For a modest fee, instructors will detail basic discipline and housetraining techniques, health and nutrition facts, and explain how a puppy learns and understands. This knowledge will enable the owner to establish his or her place as leader and gain control over the puppy from the start. This is vital, as a dog will try to take control if an owner does not effectively assume the place of leader vacated by the dam. The classes also aid in the socialization process by exposing the puppy to other people and dogs. Puppy-to-puppy socialization at an early age will have a lasting effect—reducing the dog's natural tendency as an adult to react aggressively and competitively when encountering another dog on the street or in the veterinarian's office. This early puppy training will also instill an eagerness for learning and a feeling of self-confidence in the dog.

The first few weeks in a new home are critical for both pet and owner. Talk to the supplier of your dog for information on what the puppy has been fed, its habits, what it has been taught, if it has shown fear toward anything, what it favors in a toy, etc. Try to make the transition from litter to home as painless as possible by making life as similar as possible during the early days.

To lift and support a puppy properly, place one hand against the rib cage and the other beneath the rear legs.

With proper training, this well-bred, good looking Labrador pup will grow up to be an excellent worker and loving companion.

While Labrador retrievers can vary in size and color, they all share a loving personality, a strong bond of loyalty to their people, and an irresistible zest for fun and adventure.

HOW-TO:
Helping Your Puppy Get Settled

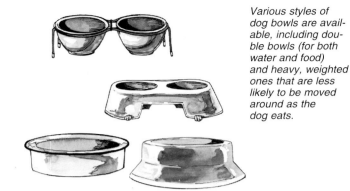

Various styles of dog bowls are available, including double bowls (for both water and food) and heavy, weighted ones that are less likely to be moved around as the dog eats.

While leaving littermates is a traumatic event in a young puppy's life, the Labrador retriever is such a gregarious, people-oriented breed that it can quickly adapt to a life surrounded by humans—even if they don't speak the same language.

Things You Will Need

You will need to have some basic supplies on hand before bringing the puppy home:
- water and food bowls
- puppy food (preferably what it has already been eating)
- bed or crate
- grooming brush
- collar and lead
- safe chew toys

Give your puppy lots of attention and encouragement during the first few days in a new home.

The First Few Days

During the first few days in the new home a lot of information will be imprinted in your dog's mind about how you feel about it. You should aim to make the transition as stress-free as possible. It is optimal to pick up a puppy from the breeder at a time when you have several days free to devote to indoctrinating your pet to its new home (such as early Saturday morning, so the immediate family can be around the puppy over the course of the weekend).

Speak to the new puppy in soft, mellow tones and gently caress it. This is not a time for roughhousing—there are many years ahead for that. At this time you need to be reassuring, comforting, and encouraging.

When the puppy arrives at its new home, let it roam and explore (within the limits of safety). Show it where the food and water dishes are kept and give it its first visit to the elimination area. Allow the puppy to set the pace, and remember that some rest periods are necessary.

Every puppy should have its own sleeping area, preferably a sleeping box or crate, to which it will be confined whenever not under direct supervision until reliably housebroken (more on crating and housebreaking later). Allow your puppy to sniff and investigate the area around its new "den." Whenever it shows signs of tiring, return it to the sleeping area and pet it until it falls asleep. This, and a lot of affection, will instill a sense of belonging in the puppy and help it to feel secure during a very insecure time.

Keep the activities limited the first few days so as not to over-stimulate or tire the puppy. Introduce only the immediate members of the household to the puppy—save the neighbors and any other household pets for supervised meetings in a few days.

The First Few Weeks

During the first weeks in a new home, a puppy should be introduced to the wonders of the world, but in a supervised manner. Experiences during these critical weeks are often permanently embedded, so it is imperative to keep the puppy from being frightened or terrorized, whether it be by neighborhood dogs, exuberant children, or loud noises such as the vacuum cleaner.

At this age the puppy should be kept occupied with mastering the initial lessons of living among humans—the pros and the cons. This should be a time of great affection toward the dog to let it know it belongs, as well as the time of its first initiation into learning *people style.* A puppy's dam has already taught it a few lessons in behavior, so do not think it is too young to learn.

A young puppy cannot be expected to master training routines, but a considerable amount of learning takes place at this time and is permanently remembered. A young puppy's attention span is short, so do not overload it or expect too much. At this point the puppy should not have developed any

bad habits, so it is a good time to begin teaching basic manners. Through careful monitoring and positive corrections a new owner can see to it that the puppy does not get the chance to go too far astray from what is required to become a reliable pet.

When the Puppy Is Alone

Should the puppy whimper or cry during the first few nights or when it is left alone for *short* periods during the day, you may want to help ease its tension by playing some soft, soothing music. I stress that the puppy should be left for only *short* periods because it should not be expected to remain alone for great lengths of time while so young. It will feel abandoned and this will affect the bonding response the animal has with its owners. In response to loneliness a puppy may also develop undesirable habits, such as tension-chewing or scratching—the effects of which will no doubt further hurt

the human-dog relationship.

If you must go out, take the puppy with you if at all possible. If this is impossible, arrange to leave the puppy with a willing substitute. Perhaps you could have someone come into your home several times during the day to socialize with the puppy, feed and exercise it, and take it to its proper elimination area. Many older school-age children will find this a fun part-time job. You will only need to give the puppy such extra-special attention for a few months, until the time when it is physically mature enough to handle an extended confinement. New owners will need to extend themselves more to see to it that their puppy is well cared for and nurtured during a critical stage of its life.

Things will get easier as the dog matures, but bear in mind that experiences during these few weeks are the ones that most affect the dog's personality in later life. A lonely puppy often grows into a maladjusted adult, and little can be done later to counteract a poor beginning.

My Tip: If you decide to hire a teenager to help with the daily care, be sure he or she is aware of proper handling of a puppy. With their natural exuberance, children frequently exhaust or overexcite their young charges.

When selecting or constructing a sleeping or whelping box, be sure it is large enough for a fully grown Labrador to lie down in comfortably.

These young Labs wait attentively for their chance to retrieve.

Note that the trainer is nearby to monitor all that happens.

Early Training Games

You can begin some elementary retrieving exercises at eight weeks or so, and your Labrador will most likely love the game and look forward to it each day. To teach the basic mechanics of the fetch (run out, pick up the object, return the object to the master, and release), begin by placing the puppy on a 10-foot lead. Take a favorite toy or a ball large enough not to be swallowed, dangle it in front and above the dog's head to gain its attention, and toss it 5 to 6 feet in front of you. Precede your command with your dog's name. For example, say, "Jake, fetch!" As he races for the toy, follow behind him. Make sure the lead stays loose and does not snap shut and frighten or hurt him (and perhaps permanently sour him on retrieving).

If he picks up the toy, praise him encouragingly. Should he merely eye or paw the toy, make him pick it up by shaking it in front of him, repeating "Jake, fetch!" Once he has grasped the toy, walk backwards to your beginning spot. Coax him to follow you by motioning him toward you using your hands and fingers. When he arrives back, get the toy from his mouth by commanding "Out!" and gently pulling it loose. Now is the time to give him a lot of praise and affection—not *during* the exercise, although encouragement can be helpful.

At such a young age, the emphasis in this and all types of exercise is on fun, not on performance. Improvement in response should naturally come with familiarity. As the puppy masters the game, vary it. Keep the dog guessing. Try to remain in position and not move out toward the toy. Later, you can attach a longer lead and extend the distance of your throw, or throw the toy sideways. Any Labrador retriever worth its name will take easily and eagerly to this game.

My Tip: Play with the puppy often and consciously make an effort to get down to its level. Standing upright, humans can be quite an imposing sight for a puppy. Sitting or lying on the floor, they are no longer towers but friendly companions. Giving a puppy some eye-to-eye attention will go a long way in cementing the human-dog bond.

These dogs have been taught to retrieve a training dummy.

Initiation to Outdoor Activities

Because Labrador retrievers make good swimmers as adults, some misinformed people think this gives them the liberty to dunk young puppies into any available pool of water. A Labrador is a natural swimmer, but the dog needs to learn the fundamentals before being expected to feel at ease in the water. When a puppy's first exposure to the water is being thrown or forced in, the shock may make it dislike and fear the water throughout life. Many potential field dogs have been ruined by improper or overzealous training.

The first introduction to the water can begin while a puppy is quite young (three months is a good age). A puppy should be able to master the mechanics very quickly, especially if "shown the ropes" by some older dogs. The owner should always be nearby, should trouble arise. It often helps the dog feel at ease if the owner wades into the water with it on the first dip.

Ponds or lakes, with their easy entries, are best for training water dogs. The slick tiles and steep sides of a pool are often unmanageable for the dog, and many drownings have occurred when an exhausted dog was unable to climb out of the water. Similarly, a young puppy is not strong enough to manage a rough ocean surf, but should be encouraged to play along the shoreline in a sheltered area of shallow water.

Once the puppy can swim with ease (and it is amazing how little time this takes), you can initiate water-retrieval exercises by throwing a small dummy into the water for the dog to try to grasp and return. Limit such exercises to just a few attempts, and praise the dog highly for every good effort. It is always important to keep in mind that these early experiences must he fun—never exhausting or frightening. Such negative experiences could spoil the dog's potential for water work as an adult.

Labradors are powerful swimmers—a skill aided by the webbing between their toes and naturally water-repellent coat.

Housebreaking

Just the sound of the word "housebreaking" gives many novice dog owners a sense of dread or a case of the jitters, but handled correctly this process can be taught quickly (if you are an efficient teacher and your Labrador is a good learner), or within a few weeks at most. Early success depends on your knowing when the dog will have to eliminate, paying attention, and being able to get the dog out in time. (Guess who else is trained simultaneously!) A puppy needs to eliminate many times a day: after waking, after eating, after strenuous play—these are definite. There are also in-between times when the puppy looks uneasy, sniffs, and walks in circles as if searching for something. Until three to six months of age, a puppy cannot physically "hold it." Bladder control is not yet established. Being alert to your dog's needs and the physical signs it gives will aid tremendously in housebreaking.

The Labrador retriever is a naturally clean breed. Labradors, like other descendants of the pack animal, want to keep their den area clean. This desire has most likely already been instilled in your puppy by its mother while she was nursing the litter. Once she no longer takes responsibility for cleaning up after each puppy's eliminations by ingesting them, she generally makes it quite clear that she wants elimination done away from the sleeping area. The puppies learn quickly to comply, or suffer a motherly correction. If your puppy came from a kennel that allowed the dam to raise the litter until weaned (aided, of course, by the twice-daily cleaning of the litter's sleeping quarters by the owner), your puppy quite possibly already knows that some areas are acceptable for eliminating and others aren't. You need to pick up where the dam left off.

Elimination is a necessary function and it should be dealt with rationally and with a good dose of common sense. Until a puppy truly understands what it is expected to do, accidents will happen. These accidents are not evidence of willful misbehavior and should therefore not be reason for punishment. React in a manner the puppy will understand. i.e., correct as the dam would correct: swiftly, firmly, fairly. Show displeasure ("No," and an angry look should suffice). Then give the puppy a clear indication of what proper procedure is by taking the dog to the elimination area and praising it. Never hit the dog or rub its nose in the excrement. Such acts are humiliating and confusing to the Labrador and totally counterproductive.

Gaining control of the bodily functions takes the dog approximately six months, so be prepared for clean-ups.

My Tip: To avoid having a stain that reattracts the dog to the spot, thoroughly clean each "accident" site with a solution designed to remove urine odor (available at pet shops or from veterinarians) or with a soapy solution containing a little vinegar. Using an ammonia-based cleaner will only enhance the problem because it is an ammonia compound in the urine that attracts the dog to the spot in the first place.

When you discover an unwanted deposit on your floor, first of all do not overreact. You want to let the dog know you are displeased, but you must do this in a manner that the dog will understand. To try to make a connection in the dog's mind with the waste, bring the dog to the spot. Have it look at the excrement, point at it, and scold in a low, growling tone. Immediately put the dog outside in the proper elimination spot. When you both return to the house, banish the dog to its crate or sleeping area for a short "time out" and then clean up the mess out of the dog's sight. It may sound silly, but cleaning up, and generally raising a fuss about it, are not the actions of a leader—in a dog's mind, at least. Correcting and banishing are. In this way the dog will comprehend your disapproval even if it wasn't directly caught in the act.

Aiding the Task

In the beginning, a puppy should be taken out almost hourly during waking hours for a chance to eliminate. Be patient. Things will get better. The number of required walks will gradually diminish to three a day when the dog reaches maturity, but it is foolhardy to rush a puppy along. The end result will be a chronic, high-strung house soiler. Another "quick-fix" to avoid is just opening the door and sending the puppy out alone, even if your yard is fenced. The puppy may not accomplish its mission, having enjoyed a romp outside instead, and it will later be forced to relieve itself inside—undoubtedly incurring the wrath of the owner, who "just took it out for a walk." You need to be with the puppy to instruct it on where to go and to keep its mind on its task, but,

most importantly, you need to be there to praise. Praise is the most effective teaching tool the owner has.

Limiting the puppy's access to unsupervised areas is a must until it is reliably housebroken. If it is allowed the run of the house, it will not regard this vast terrain as off-limits. Establish a clear area that is the dog's sleeping quarters and a clear area that is for elimination—hopefully outdoors, rather than on papers spread inside the house (see page 21). Bring the puppy to the elimination spot each time it needs to go and praise each success. Correct each mistake firmly but fairly, and immediately take the puppy to the proper spot. This is the backbone of the housebreaking process.

My Tip: The owner can help the housebreaking cause by feeding the puppy its prescribed amount of food on a regular schedule (no snacks) and by taking up the water bowl at night. These two easy steps will help to regulate the dog's elimination needs and help you to predict when the puppy must go. Maintaining a consistent schedule of feeding and walking will help prevent untimely mistakes.

Crates

Crating a puppy is by far the most efficient method of housebreaking and should not be regarded as cruel and inhumane. Crates can be purchased from most pet shops and are generally made of a heavy wire mesh or heavy-duty plastic. The crate should be large enough to allow an adult Labrador to sit up or lie down stretched out. I prefer the wire crate as it affords the dog better visibility. Undoubtedly, humans will initially think of a crate as a prison, but a dog is not a human. A dog regards its crate as its den, which is comforting. And a den is definitely something to be kept clean.

Used in conjunction with a regular schedule of walks and feedings, a crate is a valuable tool—but it cannot be abused. Once in the crate, the puppy will try not to soil its den, to the best of its ability (which isn't much). If left crated for long stretches of time, a puppy will be forced to relieve itself. This defeats the purpose of a crate. The owner must take the puppy from its crate at regular intervals and walk it to the proper spot, enthusiastically praising each success (Labradors thrive on praise).

While growing, the puppy will need to be fed three times a day (at approximately 7:00 A.M., 12:00 noon, and 5:00 P.M.) and walked very frequently (immediately upon waking, after every meal, midmorning, midafternoon, early evening, and the last thing before bedtime). All except the last walk should be followed by a play period. The puppy can then be crated for brief periods between the walks. During the first cratings it is helpful if you remain in the same room with the dog, but go about your business and pay no attention to it unless there are signs of serious distress. Hovering around the crate or apologizing to the dog for crating it is counterproductive and may make the dog unnecessarily anxious.

The maximum time allowed in the crate will depend on age. The first cratings should only be for five to ten minutes. This period should be increased slowly. During the daytime, puppies under 12 weeks of age may be crated for one hour, puppies 12 to 16 weeks may be left for two hours, and older puppies may stay a maximum of three to four hours. The dog will sleep during this time. All ages can be crated overnight. Be alert for signs of discomfort in your dog, as an individual dog may not be able to maintain this general time schedule.

The crate should be located somewhere out of the direct stream of household traffic, but not so isolated as to make the dog feel totally alone. Some owners move the crate to a corner of their bedroom at night for the extra security this imparts to the puppy, but this should not continue more than a night or two unless you are willing to accept such closeness permanently. You can place a blanket or towel on the floor of the crate and allow one chew toy inside. Do not place food or water bowls in a training crate.

As the dog matures and gains control of its elimination, the time it is confined to the crate can be reduced. Many owners will find that even after housebreaking has been mastered, the dog likes to return to the open crate for naps.

Confinement and Tethering

For those who choose not to crate their puppy, I offer two methods that extend the concept a bit. The effect should be approximately the same, although the route is less direct. Instead of crating between walks, confine the puppy to a small, "mistakeproof" (i.e., uncarpeted) room or, alternatively, tether the dog to you by a short lead.

To confine an increasingly agile and curious Labrador retriever puppy within its assigned place, use a mesh baby gate to block off the escape route. Avoid the older triangular wood gates, which can be dangerous as the puppy can get its head caught in the holes. One distinct problem with using a gate is that your nimble Labrador will quickly be able to jump or climb over it, which forces you to put a second gate on top of the first, or to devise a better Labrador trap.

The second technique—tying the dog directly to you—is a bit drastic and should be reserved for sneaky repeat offenders who leave "surprises" where and when you least expect them. Simply place the dog on its lead, tie the lead to your belt loop or

With proper training, your Labrador puppy should be reliably housetrained in a few weeks, but expect some "accidents" now and then from even the best behaved dog.

wrist, and have the dog follow you wherever you go. You can be assured that while using this technique you will know when the dog has made a mistake, or is about to. You will then be right in position to provide immediate correction and get the dog to the proper spot. This method may be quite cumbersome, but it can yield results quickly. Labradors are very intelligent dogs and no self-respecting Labrador could tolerate such overbearing leadership for long without catching on to what is tolerated and what is not.

Paper Training

If an owner cannot be with the puppy during the day, housebreaking must be done by means of paper training. It is certainly the slowest method, and the messiest, but for those who find it necessary it will do the job.

Despite good intentions, a puppy confined to a crate cannot keep its den clean for the entire day. This does not, however, mean that such a puppy cannot benefit from a crate. During the times you are at home, use the crate method as described above but utilize papers as the proper elimination area. When away, leave the dog with a supply of papers near, but not under, the *opened* crate. In this way the puppy can use the papers when necessary, and still pass the time napping in the crate.

Confine the dog to a limited space and divide the room into three areas: the elimination area, the crate or sleeping area, and the feeding area. The papers should be several layers thick and should not extend to the other territories. To familiarize the puppy with using the papers, place it on the papers when you know it needs to eliminate and encourage it with "Do your business," or some similar phrase that does not include such terms as *come, sit, down,* etc., which will be introduced soon in basic obedience training. When it catches on, lavish the dog with praise to reinforce the notion that this site is acceptable.

A paper-trained dog should be retrained to use the outdoors at five to six months of age. At this point in its development, it should show signs of greater retention and may make it through the day without the need to eliminate.

My tip: Walk the dog just before leaving for the day and immediately upon your return. Your Labrador will be able to adjust to waiting all day as quickly as its system will allow, so be patient and encouraging.

Cleaning Up After Your Dog

Upon depositing its wastes, the dog never gives them another thought. It is up to the owner to take care of the cleanup. In many cities and states across America it is now mandatory to pick up solid waste excreted by pets in public areas. Those who do not comply face fines ranging from $25 to $100. Thoughtful owners should clean up after their pets because this not only rids the streets and public areas of potentially harmful (and certainly repugnant) material, but it also shows that dog owners as a whole are

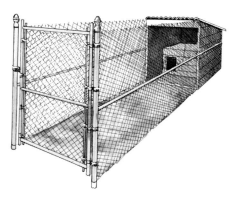

This dog house and run combination is ideal for Labrador retrievers. It provides ample room for exercise and an escape-proof housing area.

responsible people who do not inflict their pets on non-dog-lovers. Without such care, apartment dwellers will find it increasingly hard to find housing that will allow pets, and more and more landlords and city officials will ban dogs from their buildings and grounds. It is easier to stoop and scoop (a tissue and an inverted plastic bag covering your hand are all you need) than to give up a way of life.

Kenneling

A well-rounded gun dog will love both the outdoors and its hunting family. From an early age, such dogs should spend a considerable amount of their time experiencing the outdoors and the kennel. From the time they can walk, they should be allowed as much time as possible in the yard, digging the dirt and running through all sorts of terrain in all sorts of weather. They should also be socialized to enjoy the companionship of humans as well as kennel mates.

If a litter of puppies is to be reared in a kennel building rather than in the house, you must be sure this building is adequately temperature controlled. This is most important during the cold

A cutaway view of a dog house. When properly insulated this shelter provides a comfortable sleeping spot as well as protection from the extremes of weather. The top is hinged to allow for easy cleaning.

months. As the pups mature, they will be able to withstand the cold with typical Labrador hardiness, but puppies must be carefully sheltered in warm, dry surroundings. If the kennel is not adequately heated for the needs of puppies, keep them in the house the first winter and teach them how to live outside in the spring. A little added socialization will do them good, anyway.

Outdoor runs and housing should always provide the dog with adequate shelter from all climatic extremes (heat, cold, wind, rain, etc.). While intended to confine, such housing should be spacious enough to allow unrestricted movement and a chance for exercise as well.

My Tip: If you are planning a combination doghouse and fenced run, be aware that Labradors can be proficient climbers. They have been known to scale a fence by using the doghouse roof as a jumping point. To eliminate this possibility, plan to have a raised roof over the house; alternatively, have the house located *outside* the run by placing the entrance to the house flush against the fence and having an entrance hole cut into the fence. In this way the run and house are connected, yet the dog has no access to the roof and no space inside the run is taken up by the house.

Since many Labradors are quite adept at climbing, use a *minimum* height of 5 feet (1.5 m) for any fencing. To prevent escape under the fence, bury it 12 inches deep (30 cm)

to thwart avid diggers. The house must be thoroughly insulated, draft-proof, and set on a proper foundation. A dirt floor is cold, damp, unhealthy, and impossible to keep clean.

Remember: A kennel-raised dog often bonds most closely to the one person who spends the most time with it, generally the trainer who will also be the hunting partner. It is vital that the dog also be allowed some time away from the kennel to socialize with new people and other animals. In this way the dog's natural temperament is allowed to develop normally. Dogs that live in kennels and only see a trainer for brief periods develop "kennel vision" and often become misfits in situations that well-socialized dogs thrive in. At the other extreme, dogs that were strictly home-raised and then transferred to the kennel life often suffer emotionally by being deprived of the companionship they have grown to need.

Labrador retrievers make good kennel dogs and get along well with their kennelmates. Fighting is rare. To thrive in such a situation (which incidentally was the way the breed was kept for nearly a hundred years, before they also became house pets), a kennel dog must be well taken care of. With proper attention, a kennel dog will not be neurotic, lonely, or aggressive. When provided with a well-ventilated, well-lit, clean, and comfortable environment, the Labrador will thrive—as long as the owner-handler tends to the dog's social needs as well.

Various types of traveling containers and crates are available from pet shops and distributors. They are essential when you and your Labrador are using public transportation.

Travel by Car

Since your Labrador may sometimes accompany you when you travel, it is important to indoctrinate it into riding in the car while it is still a puppy. Start with short trips, such as local errands, and increase from there. The dog should always ride in the back seat and should be taught to lie down while the car is moving. Young puppies often do well to ride in their crates during any extended car trip.

For trips of more than an hour, do not feed the dog just prior to departure. Like people, many dogs experience motion sickness. Should your dog be prone to vomiting in the car, it will require medication from your veterinarian whenever you are

Train your Labrador retriever to lie down in the back seat while the car is moving.

planning a long drive. Most dogs outgrow this as they get more accustomed to car trips. Plan on stopping at least every two hours, at which time you should walk the dog to give it some exercise and a chance to relieve itself. Remember that the dog will be in an unfamiliar terrain, so always have it on leash to prevent an unexpected bolting.

While the car is moving, allow a small amount of fresh air to circulate inside by opening the windows approximately 2 inches (5 cm) from the top. This should be sufficient, as large doses of air from fully opened windows can cause eye, ear, and throat irritation.

Caution: In the summertime, provide several small amounts of drinking water during the trip to prevent dehydration. When stopped, *never leave a dog in a parked car during the heat of the day.* Even with the windows slightly lowered, the internal temperature of the car can soar in just minutes and be fatal to the dog.

If you are planning an extended trip requiring overnight lodging, make reservations in advance at a hotel or motel that

will allow pets. Travel guides or your local automobile club should be able to supply you with a list of places that accept animals.

Boarding Your Lab: If you are to be away and must leave your Labrador behind, the most satisfactory arrangement would be to leave the dog with a friend or relative with whom the dog is familiar. Barring this, you have several options. The breeder from whom you purchased your dog may have the facilities to house it on a temporary basis. Alternatively, you can check your local papers for "foster care" advertisements by local people who are willing to look after pets in their home for a limited amount of time. Should you consider this method, be sure to visit the site on several occasions with the dog to familiarize it with the people and location and to verify that this is a suitable environment for your pet. Commercial kennels offer boarding services for those with no other options. Most kennels are clean and tend to all your pet's basic needs, but Labradors are very people-oriented and tend to miss the companionship they are used to when placed in boarding kennels. Should this be necessary, however, check that the kennel is accredited by the American Boarding Kennel Association. A list of approved kennels in your area can be obtained by writing ABKA at 4575 Galley Road, Suite 400A, Colorado Springs, CO 80915.

Travel by Air

In recent years air travel for animals has become much safer due to new airline regulations that require animals to be shielded from all extremes of temperature and pressure. Traveling in airplanes has become almost routine procedure for show dogs or for planned matings that involve partners from different areas of the country.

For a nominal fee, most airlines will provide an appropriate crate for shipping the dog, if you do not own one. Consult with your airline well ahead of departure time for any specific requirements the airline may have for arrival times or unloading procedures. To protect against a potentially tragic mix-up (airlines have been known to lose luggage, haven't they?), mark the outside of the

When preparing for a trip, be sure to pack all the essentials: collar and lead, a sturdy dish, some type of bedding, and a supply of the dog's regular food.

traveling crate with "Live Animal" and the name, address, and phone number of both the shipper and the scheduled receiver. Include another copy of this information inside the crate with the dog.

To help insure a comfortable trip, place a blanket at the bottom of the crate. Exercise the dog and be sure it has relieved itself before placing it in the crate. If at all possible, stay with the crate until you see it taken for loading.

It is vital to take or send along with the dog a supply of its usual food for the time it is to be out of its normal home environment. New places and faces can be stressful enough without adding a risk of digestive upset by forcing the dog to eat an unfamiliar diet.

At the airport, you may be required to muzzle your dog when it is not in the crate. Be sure to choose a muzzle made of strong leather that has a strap across the forehead.

Feeding Your Labrador

Selecting the right food for your Labrador retriever should not be a haphazard choice, as no other decision will have a greater impact on the overall well-being of your dog. What the dog eats affects its nutrition, and nutrition directly relates to overall health and longevity. A dog's diet should be high in protein. with an ample supply of carbohydrates, fat, vitamins, and minerals. These requirements are easily met by selecting *nutritionally complete* products.

Most single-pet households purchase their dog's food from the supermarket. Often, pet owners are swayed into trying certain brands by price, packaging, and advertising (humans will be humans); but the most popular brands may not be the best buys for your dog.

Types of Food

There are three main types of dog food: canned, semimoist, and dry; plus the old standby, table scraps. Each of these used as the sole diet presents problems. A diet consisting exclusively of canned and semimoist foods can wreak havoc with a dog's digestive system, teeth, and gums. Some dry foods must be taken in massive amounts to obtain all of the nutrients that are essential. And table scraps can throw a well-balanced diet right out of kilter. However, in spite of these pitfalls, there is no reason to despair. With a little research (read labels and compare), and perhaps some trial and error, you should be able to work out the proper balanced diet for your dog.

Canned Food

Canned dog food should never be served as the sole food. First of all, it is very high in water content (approximately 75 percent) and you end up paying hefty prices for little real substance. The meat used in canned food is certainly not from choice cuts, either, so don't let evasive television commercials fool you into thinking canned food is optimal. The additives commonly used in canned foods, such as coloring and preservatives, are basically nondigestible by the dog and can have a diuretic effect. Add this to the high water content and you will understand why a dog eating primarily canned food will have an increased need for urination and potential housebreaking problems.

There are some canned foods that are better than others, however, notably the ones designed for the different stages of a dog's life. Even these should make up no more than one-quarter of the dog's daily intake and should be used in conjunction with a quality meat/meal-based dry food.

Semimoist Food

The semimoist foods are usually packaged in easy-open pouches or as "hamburger patties." They are an expensive convenience food—convenient for the owner. The semimoist foods contain much less water than canned foods, but they are loaded with sugar, preservatives, and additives that make the product attractive to the *human* eye (the dogs couldn't care less). These materials can sometimes produce allergic reactions that commonly result in skin biting or scratching by the sensitive dog.

Again, there are some semimoists that are more nutritious than others, but I would recommend limiting such products to no more than one-quarter of the diet, with the remaining three-quarters being a quality dry food.

Dry Food

The dry-food category spans a large spectrum of quality. For purposes of distinction, I break it into two types: commercial and professional. Most of the popular brands in supermarkets fall into the first category. The main problem with these is the amount the dog needs to consume daily in order to attain proper nutrition. Often, it is just too much, and leads to excessive elimination. Check the recommended feeding amounts on the bag and apply it to your dog's weight. If the suggested amount turns out to be more than your dog can easily eat in one meal, choose another brand. A second drawback of this type of dry food is that the mixture of ingredients often varies from batch to batch, due to fluctuations in which crop—soy, wheat, oats, etc.—is available at what time. Therefore, the nutritional value may differ somewhat from bag to bag.

The "professional" meat-meal blends offer some improvement. These are the high-quality dry foods sold primarily in pet shops and specialty stores. They offer a nutritious, balanced diet in an easily digestible form. The makers retain a standard blending procedure from batch to batch to insure a uniform product. The suggested feeding amounts are adequate to fill a dog up without overfeeding. Although such products may cost a little more, in the long run they are no more expensive than brands that require more to be eaten. A quality meat-meal-based dry food has also been shown to aid in the housebreak-

ing process as this type of mixture usually contains bran or fiber in amounts that help to produce firmer stools. (Dry foods without such fiber are also more apt to be lacking in texture. When chewed they are likely to stick to the roof of the dog's mouth.)

Some people feel that the dry foods are too low in fat content. This is easily handled by adding one-half can of canned food, if so desired, or, as an alternative, add ½ to 1½ teaspoons corn, safflower, or canola (rapeseed) oil to the ration once or twice weekly.

Supplementation

Adding things to a dog's basic diet will often do more harm than good. Giving your dog an occasional snack—dog biscuits, an apple, a carrot—is fine in moderation. Dogs need roughage, too, but overdoing can cause nutri-

All dogs should always have plenty of fresh, clean water available at all times. This is especially important when the diet consists mainly of dry food.

Not only are there many types of food to select from, there are also quality differences between brands. Read the labels to make sure the food you give your Labrador is of the highest quality and fulfills all daily requirements.

tional upset. Keep in mind that high-quality commercial foods are intended to contain all your dog needs.

Table Scraps

Put table scraps where they belong—in the garbage, not in the dog's bowl. Many people think that giving Jake that nice chunk of fat from their sirloin will add luster to his coat. While it may put joy in Jake's heart, it may also give him loose bowels. An occasional veal bone, if very sturdy (a knuckle, for example), can give Jake a tooth cleaning and some jaw exercise, but be careful, since most bones are constipating as well as dangerous (an ingested splinter of bone can be fatal).

Nylon or rawhide "bones" are safest. They are available in most pet stores, groceries, and supermarkets.

If you want to give your dog more than his everyday food (even though dogs generally do not get bored with their meals, unlike humans), try *small amounts* of fruits, cereal, and vegetables. They do not upset the intestinal tract by their oiliness or indigestibility, and actually promote effective digestion. You may also try well-trimmed (no visible fat) bits of meat. However, a dog raised on snacks of sirloin tips will not take kindly to a change to vegetables, so pursue this course with considerable caution.

Vitamins and Coat Enhancers

Unless prescribed by your veterinarian for a specific condition, do not give your dog vitamin supplements. A dog only needs small amounts of vitamins and minerals. True, they play an important role in development, but the necessary quantities are contained in almost every commercial dog food. Overdoing by supplementation is much more common than a vitamin deficiency—and can be more damaging.

In trying to get an edge in the show ring, some people resort to "coat enhancers" and the like. While this may aid long-coated breeds, the Labrador's coarse, dense coat is primarily controlled by the quality of its genes, not its diet, so such tonics are usually ineffective. A well-balanced diet should keep a healthy Labrador retriever in proper condition, provided that adequate exercise is also supplied.

The Feeding Process

While deciding *what* to feed your Labrador retriever certainly is the top priority, *how, when,* and *where* are also vital aspects. Once you resolve all these issues, you should set the pattern for a healthful lifestyle for your dog.

Where you feed your dog is important. In many households you will find Jake being fed right in the middle of the kitchen floor, probably at a time when the kitchen is in full use. People, thinking in their human way, naturally feel that the dog appreciates being part of the family scene and enjoys sharing meals with the family. But dogs are animals with pack instincts, not humans. They should be allowed to eat their meal in peace, without having to entertain thoughts of whether anyone is going to try to take their food away from them. Many dogs gulp down their food not as a result of hunger but out of a desire to finish quickly before they are disturbed. (They often vomit this food back up and eat it a second time, which is an unappetizing process for humans to watch but quite normal for dogs.) As mild mannered as Labrador retrievers are, they do not appreciate interruptions and will eat better if fed each day in a private area, out of the flow of traffic.

When to feed your Labrador is generally a matter of choice and the age of the dog. Young puppies require four or five small meals a day. From about four to eight months, the growing puppy will need three meals a day: morning, noon, and night. Reduce the feeding schedule to two meals a day at about nine months of age, and finally to the adult diet of one large meal a day at 11 or 12 months of age. Most owners feed an adult dog its main meal in the late afternoon or early evening, and often augment this with a few biscuits or some kibble in the morning. (Could you really go 24 hours on one meal?) Others just divide the rations into two smaller feedings. Use whatever suits you and your dog best.

How you feed your Labrador refers not only to the method but also to *how much.* There is no set amount that will apply to every Labrador retriever, and product-label directions should only be used as guides. Quite naturally, the size, age, temperament (active or lazy), and amount of daily exercise will dictate the number of calories needed. The primary indicator of how well a dog is being fed is its overall trim. A Labrador retriever should be firm, not plump. It is easy for today's dogs to get out of condition by not exercising enough and by being fed too much by well-meaning owners (we humans often equate food with love). Labradors will overeat if encouraged, so don't let Jake nibble to his liking from a perpetually full bowl. At the other extreme, if the ribs and hipbones can be easily felt upon running your hand down the dog's side, your pet may require additional calories. Telltale signs of undernourishment are a lack of coat sheen and an overall malaise. Labradors are normally peppy, so a physical slowdown should be carefully monitored.

Remember: As a dog ages, it will need less food to maintain a constant weight. With elderly dogs it is important to cut back on the amount of protein (particularly meat) that is ingested, as high levels of protein can put a strain on the kidneys.

Overweight dogs should be brought back into trim, primarily through gradually increasing their daily exercise. Cut back on the number of calories in the dog's diet by substituting low-calorie fillers (such as grated carrot or apples, unsalted popped corn, or low-fat cottage cheese) for a portion of their meal.

Underweight dogs can be brought up to trim by adding high-calorie boosters to their meals, such as an occasional raw egg, cheese, or hamburger. Such caloric supplementation may also be needed during the winter if your Labrador is kenneled or worked outside much of the time, and during peak working periods when extra calories are burned. A high-calorie supplement, such as Nutri-Cal, can be purchased in squeeze tubes from your veterinarian.

On the whole, Labradors are not problem eaters. They like to eat. (In

Healthy
Labradors are the
end-product of a
nutritious diet,
plentiful exercise,
and regular
grooming.

my opinion, problem eaters are the result of problem feeders—the owners.) By keeping the feeding process a simple routine, there should be no fuss. Allow the dog its privacy, and give it ample time to complete its meal (approximately 15 to 20 minutes). After this time, pick up and discard whatever food is left in the bowl. Adjust the amount given each day until the dog will clean its bowl. If the dog is still eating when you come to retrieve the bowl, allow another five minutes.

When a dog refuses to eat its meal, *do not* offer it anything else until the next scheduled meal. Giving in and trying to please a fussy eater only enhances and entrenches the problem. Don't worry, Jake will not starve even if he misses a meal or two. You may want to change the diet *once* if the refusal continues for several days and the dog seems outwardly healthy and hungry. The food may really be distasteful to the dog (as I mentioned, some companies do change their formulas without notice), but most dogs are not that particular. A sudden disaffection with food may be a physical or a behavioral problem. The food is most likely all right. This may be a good time to bring Jake in for a checkup. If all is well, your leadership is being tested. (Don't be offended; dogs will be dogs.) Above all, don't whine or nag the dog to eat. Simply place the dog in its assigned feeding site, give it the food, and leave it alone. It will give in when it figures out that you won't, and should eat well from then on.

My Tip: There are some additional do's and don'ts concerning feeding:
• Keep an ample supply of fresh water available at all times. This is especially important during hot weather, when active dogs can become dehydrated.
• Clean the water and food bowls with hot water and a mild detergent each day to inhibit the growth of bacteria, which can cause intestinal problems.

• When traveling or if the dog is kenneled for any reason, bring along a supply of the dog's regular food.
• Don't make wholesale changes in a dog's diet, as this can cause digestive upset. Make any necessary changes slowly.
• Don't leave the water bowl out all night if the dog is having any housebreaking accidents during the night.
• Don't serve cold (refrigerated) canned food. Make sure it is at room temperature.

Teething and Chewing

Dogs need and like to chew. Realizing this and preparing for it may save your leather shoes or prevent the shredding of your daughter's favorite doll (and let me tell you from family experience that this is truly unpleasant for all involved).

A puppy will chew to help cut its first teeth, to exercise its jaws, to strengthen its bite, to rid itself of those first teeth, and to relieve tension. In other words, a puppy does a lot of chewing, particularly from four to nine months of age when permanent teeth are emerging.

As the dog matures, the need to chew remains. Today's Labrador retriever is fed a diet that is all but predigested—there is little real texture in most dog foods, let alone enough abrasive material to clean the teeth of accumulating tartar (unless you are lucky enough to have a Labrador that likes to munch on raw carrots). If not removed, tartar buildup will irritate the gums and eventually rot the teeth at the gumline. The dog finds relief in chewing.

Chewing is also a means for the dog to relieve tension or boredom. Luckily, Labrador retrievers are not as prone to chewing when bored as other more high-strung breeds. (One case that comes to mind is a friend's Dalmatian, who was thought to be lazily taking a nap on the bed.

Actually, she was busy chewing through a down comforter and into the mattress—ouch!) Labradors, especially young ones, will often chew when lonely, however. Left alone for extended periods, dogs will resort to such destructive behavior.

There is no simple method to stop chewing, but prevention is the best course of action. During the teething stage, confine the dog when it cannot be supervised (a crate is best!) and give it something it is allowed to chew.

Warning: Do not think the teething process is over after the dog has shed its milk teeth. Teething becomes intense again at approximately eight or nine months when the molars emerge. By this time most of the earlier chewing has stopped, so many owners are unprepared for this renewed, often aggressive chewing. (Table legs are often targets.)

Whenever the dog is allowed the run of the house, be diligent about not leaving "chewables" unguarded. A dog must be taught what can and cannot be chewed, and unfortunately this lesson is learned through making mistakes—hopefully not too costly (my brother's Lab pup just chewed the custom-made venetian blinds) or deadly ones (electric cords can be fatal). When you catch your Labrador in the act of chewing a forbidden object, make it clear that this is off limits. Remove the object from the dog's clutches, shake it or tap it to draw the dog's attention to the object, and correct with "No!" Immediately give the dog its proper chew object. If the dog repeats its misdeed with the same object, add a shake of the neck to the correction and follow this with a lengthy down-stay (see page 80) or a trip to the crate to get your displeasure across. Repeat offenders should be crated whenever they are not being supervised until they catch on to proper behavior.

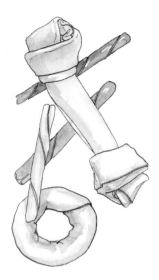

Rawhide chews should be given as a treat, but not as a regular part of the diet. Make sure the dog cannot bite off a piece so large that it can lodge in its throat.

To satisfy the chewing need, supply your Labrador retriever with a safe chewable. Don t give the dog a worn-out pair of shoes to teethe on and then expect it to leave your slippers alone. Bones are effective toothbrushes, but can be dangerous as well as constipating, so give them sparingly. Select sturdy bones that will not splinter. However, such bones may be too abrasive to tooth enamel if your dog is a prodigious chewer. The heavy nylon bones sold through pet stores are good chewables that have been specifically designed to withstand much abuse without breaking into dangerous pieces; the only drawback is that many dogs find them unappealing and won't use them. Rawhide bones are another solution, but most dogs can do away with them in short order. Many Labrador retrievers are content with a large, sturdy, hard rubber ball.

Chewing and mouthing this yielding surface can satisfy many of the chewing needs, but leaves the task of removing most of the tooth tartar to you and your veterinarian

Tooth Care

Tooth tartar, or plaque, can be a life-long problem for dogs, just as it is for humans. (And dogs don't brush after every meal and pay semiannual visits to the dental hygienist to remove accumulations.) Left unchecked, tartar will erode the dog's tooth enamel and rot away the teeth, primarily at the gumline.

The main cure and prevention of tartar buildup should come from the diet. Given something abrasive to chew (other than the venetian blinds), most dogs will need little further dental care. Training the dog while young to snack on hard vegetables, such as carrots, and an occasional veal bone will aid in keeping the teeth clean. The gnawing of the bone should be enough to remove most buildup. The naturally occurring acid that is found in such foods as tomatoes is also touted as being able to reduce tartar buildup—if you can get the dog to eat them. A surer method is to accustom your Labrador from puppyhood to having its teeth gently cleaned with a soft brush or a moistened gauze pad.

If you notice a yellowing of the tooth exterior, which is common as the dog ages, further treatment is in order. Brushing the dog's teeth once a week with a mild paste of baking soda and hydrogen peroxide or with a specialized dentifrice available from your veterinarian may remove the stain and plaque. This is accomplished by using a child's toothbrush and, if performed in a gentle but firm manner, should not be frightening or painful for the dog. If the discoloration remains after several weeks of brushing, a visit to the veterinarian for a tooth scaling is in order. A dog needs its teeth throughout life, so

Few owners bother to attend to their pet's teeth, and the result can be cavities and bad breath. You can purchase a dentifrice made especially for dogs from your veterinarian. It is designed to remove plaque and control the growth of oral bacteria.

everything must be done to prevent their loss. If the veterinarian feels that the buildup is chronic, he or she may instruct you on how to scrape away the plaque on your own as part of the dog's regular grooming schedule.

Tooth problems are often not revealed by the outward condition or color of the teeth. A sign of trouble is a sudden change in the dog's breath that persists for more than a day or two. This may indicate a problem with either the teeth or the throat. Decaying teeth will also cause the dog to go off its food. If you suspect a dental problem, inspect the mouth and gums for any sign of bleeding, swelling, or sensitivity to touch. An abscessed tooth sometimes manifests itself as a boil-like growth on the cheek area. Your veterinarian should be informed as soon as you spot any of these conditions.

Exercise

Little needs to be said about the need for adequate exercise. A Labrador retriever is a worker by heritage and should not be allowed to remain inactive and grow fat. An overweight dog will die at a much earlier age than a trim, well-conditioned dog whose heart is toned and able to cope with the appropriate amount of body weight and withstand disease. There is no need for a Labrador to be overweight, as it does not need extensive amounts of exercise to stay fit. Labradors are not hyperactive dogs needing continuous access to wide open spaces, but they must be given at least three walks a day, one of which allows for several minutes of vigorous activity. Without a proper outlet for their energy, some dogs become destructive in the home, restless, or even depressed.

Labrador retrievers can become lazy if not encouraged to exercise. Compound this problem with overfeeding, which is very common, and extra pounds are easily put on. Taking them off again is harder work, requiring a more appropriate diet and a concerted effort to increase vigorous exercise time (gradually, of course, to prevent possible muscle injury or overexertion).

Swimming and retrieving games are natural outlets for Labrador retrievers. These activities are ones that the breed excels at and enjoys, and they give a complete, full-muscle workout that tones the entire body. Having access to a swimming area may be a problem for most owners, but retrieving games can be played anywhere.

Labradors have great stamina, but owners must use common sense. During the summer months, limit strenuous exercise during the hottest part of the day and provide an ample supply of fresh water. In the winter, a Labrador in good trim should be able to withstand the cold very effectively and should not be kept housebound. If the dog is out in the rain or snow for any length of time, it should be dried off when it returns to the heated indoors.

Most Labradors will play catch with boundless energy—usually outlasting their owner's willingness to throw! They are natural fielders and adept at handling a tennis ball, stick, or frisbee.

Grooming

Coat Care

Caring for the coat of a Labrador retriever is not much of a problem. The short, dense hair is easily groomed with a daily application of a hound glove or bristle brush. The coat is basically dirt and water repellent, and seldom becomes offensive. There is little shedding, even though the Labrador loses its undercoat once or twice yearly. Coat trimming is unnecessary (although sometimes resorted to by show competitors who feel tidying is necessary to highlight this or downplay that aspect of conformation).

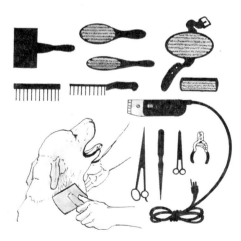

The basic grooming tools needed to keep a Labrador's coat in good condition are a wire sticker, bristle brushes, medium- and fine-tooth combs, a nail clipper, and a nail file. When trimming for a show, an electric clipper and scissors can aid in enhancing the fine lines of a potentially prize-winning specimen.

Bathing should not be a routine matter, but should only be undertaken when absolutely necessary (such as that unexpected meeting with a local skunk, a roll in the mud, or the presence of an accumulated "doggy odor" from the oils in the coat). Washing a Labrador too frequently eliminates too much of the natural oils that give the outer coat its desired harshness. Soap residue can also dry out the skin and be irritating to the dog.

Yellows may need to be bathed a little more frequently than blacks or chocolates, as their coat may pick up some discoloration from grass and dirt. This can often be taken care of by spot washing only the main contact points—the lower legs and thighs.

When bathing is needed, be sure to use a very mild soap designed especially for the dog's coat—not commercial products for humans, which are much too drying for a dog. When bathing the dog, work the water down through the dense outer coat to the skin. Afterward, be very careful to dry the dog thoroughly. It may sound silly to worry about a Labrador retriever getting a chill from a bath, when a hunting Labrador often spends many hours diving in and out of icy waters without so much as a shiver. However, the bathing process temporarily removes some of the dog's natural water-repellent oils and gets the dog wet at the skin. At this point, even a water dog is vulnerable to temperature extremes, so be cautious.

Caution: Should you notice a change in coat appearance, such as a dulling of the normal sheen, inspect the skin closely for signs of parasite infestation or other skin disorders. If the dog begins to scratch incessantly or chew its coat and skin, there is an irritation present that must be diagnosed by a competent veterinarian. Recent nutritional studies have shown that many such skin problems can be traced to allergic reactions to food additives or other substances. A change in the natural oils of the coat may point to metabolic problems involving the liver, kidneys, or the digestive tract. The loss of hair may be tied to hormonal imbalances, or could be due to infectious mange. The point is that the coat is often an indicator of general health and should not be overlooked just because the Labrador is lucky enough not to need much attention paid to it.

Eyes and Ears

After a day of hunting or a run in overgrown terrain, a Labrador retriever's eyes and ears should be inspected for signs of imbedded objects or scratches. The ear can be easily inspected with the aid of a small flashlight to help you see the upper interior. It is quite easy for burrs to become entangled in or around the ear canal, or for tiny seeds to work their way under the eyelids and irritate the eye. The dog will react to such irritants by pawing at the spot, often causing more damage by scraping the surface raw and inviting infection. If the dog is continuously rubbing these areas and no cut or imbedded object is visible, there may be an abrasion that will require a salve to remove the sting and aid in healing.

Ear troubles are also indicated when a dog constantly shakes its head, rubs its head against the ground, produces an excessive amount of visible earwax, or if there is a foul odor from the ear's interior. If the dog reacts violently to an inspection of the ear or if there is

Should something become lodged in your pet's eye or if there is a persistent discharge, inspect the eye by bracing your hands around the dog's head and separating the eyelids using gentle pressure.

redness or swelling, it probably is suffering from an inflammation called otitis that must be treated topically by your veterinarian (antibiotics are sometimes required also). Such inflammations can be the result of a variety of causes, such as parasitic mites or bacterial infections, so an accurate diagnosis is imperative.

My Tip: You should not resort to over-the-counter ointments unless guided by your veterinarian. Deafness can be the end result of mistreated ear infections.

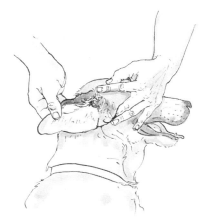

*To inspect your dog's ear, gently fold the ear back and check the outer canal for signs of excessive wax, dirt, or lodged debris. Should any signs of pus, blood, or a foul odor be present, veterinary care will be required. **Do not probe inside the ear canal.***

You can help to alleviate the normal buildup of wax and dirt in the ear by routinely swabbing the easily accessible areas of the ear with a cotton ball wet with a little warm water. Ointments made specifically for cleaning the outer ear can be purchased from pet shops, grooming parlors, or your veterinarian if cleanliness is a continual problem. Avoid oily compounds, as they may leave a sticky residue that will retain dirt. Do not probe into the ear canal during cleaning, as this can be very damaging and extremely painful for the dog. Clean only the exposed area. If you suspect that the ear is becoming clogged, bring the dog to the veterinarian for a more thorough cleaning. You should ask for instructions on how to perform this procedure at home if the problem is chronic.

To remove small amounts of discharge that may collect around the corners of the eye, carefully dab it away with a damp, clean, lint-free cloth. If the dog continues to blink excessively or if the eye is red, consult your veterinarian. Minor irritations can quickly become serious, so special attention must be paid to any tearing or discharge from these sensitive areas.

Nails and Feet

A Labrador retriever's feet are susceptible to various injuries if it spends much time outdoors. The pads of the feet should be inspected after every vigorous run in thick brush for cuts, splinters, burrs, or imbedded stones. For minor problems, a cleaning, using sterilized tweezers to remove any objects, and a mild antiseptic should be all that is needed. The dog should not be permitted any hard running until the cut is healed. Undiscovered minor irritations can quickly become infected and painful, causing the dog to favor the leg and limp. A dog that develops a sudden limp may have been stung by an insect. In such a case, an ice compress will usually reduce or prevent swelling and the pain should quickly pass. (Be alert to any difficulty in breathing, as an allergic reaction to stings may also produce dangerous side effects.) If there

Check your dog's nails regularly, as overly long nails can impede normal gait and cause foot problems. A guillotine-type nail clipper is quick and efficient.

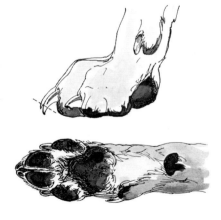

Be sure to cut the nails at a slight angle, as shown, and be careful not to cut so deeply as to injure the "quick" of the nail.

is no evidence of a cut and the dog continues to favor the leg, consult a veterinarian as there may be an injury to the bones or muscles of the foot, or something may be imbedded within the footpad that will need an experienced hand to remove.

My Tip: Because many adult dogs dislike having their feet touched or inspected, begin this as a daily routine while the dog is young.

Dogs that receive ample exercise outside the house will seldom need to have their nails trimmed, as moving about on rough surfaces should be enough to keep the nails quite short. Dogs that are more sedentary will need their nails attended to. If allowed to continue growing, the nails will impede the normal placement of the foot and affect the dog's gait.

Caution: Overgrown nails can also be dangerous as they can be ripped off, causing serious injury to the foot.

Specially designed nail clippers for medium-sized dogs such as Labrador retrievers can be purchased at most pet shops or grooming parlors. The process is quick and painless, if done properly. If you are inexperienced with this, have your veterinarian show you this simple procedure at the dog's regular checkup. From then on this can be performed at home. Be sure to cut only the outer shell of the nail, as cutting too close to the quick will cause bleeding. Once the nail is the proper length, smooth the surface with a few touches of an emery board. Should bleeding occur from the cutting, apply pressure to the area by holding a cotton swab over the nail. Once the bleeding stops, dab the nail with a mild antiseptic.

In the wintertime, if you live in the colder areas, check your dog's feet after it walks on snow-covered or shoveled sidewalks. The chemicals that are commonly applied to melt snow on walkways and roads can be caustic to your dog's skin and feet and

must be removed quickly by a thorough washing with warm, soapy water. Follow this by applying a generous amount of petroleum jelly to the footpads to soothe any discomfort. If the use of such snow-melting chemicals is common in your area, ask your veterinarian to recommend a cream that you can apply to protect the footpads before damage occurs. If this salt is allowed to remain, the pads can be chemically burned. In response to the pain the dog may try to wash the chemicals off by licking, which complicates the problem further. If ingested in large enough doses, such materials can injure the digestive tract and other organs. The same applies to anyantifreeze that may leak onto the streets. Not only is this liquid deadly, but it also actually attracts dogs by its pleasant smell and taste. Beware of letting your dog walk on or lick any liquids in the streets.

After every trip outdoors, the Labrador's feet and coat should be inspected for lodged burrs, minor cuts, and abrasions.

If Your Dog Gets Sick

I strongly recommend seeking an expert's advice whenever the state of the dog's health is in doubt. Rely on the expertise of your veterinarian instead of guessing and waiting too long to seek help for an ailing pet. Speed is often the difference between a quick or a costly solution. There are, however, some basic procedures that you can perform yourself.

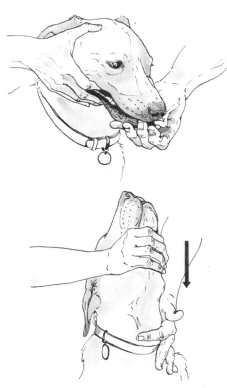

If you must administer a pill to your dog, apply slight pressure at the back of the mouth next to the molars to get the dog to open its mouth, and then insert the pill as far back as possible. Lift the dog's head slightly and rub the throat for several seconds to coax the dog to swallow.

Odds are you will have to administer medication to your dog sometime in its life. There are several methods, depending on the required type and amount. Liquid medicine should be placed in a medicine spoon or syringe and poured into the *back* of the mouth by lifting the lower lip near the back molars and holding the head *slightly* upward to let the medicine slide down the throat. If the dog tries to spit the medicine out, place your hand around the muzzle and gently hold the head until swallowing occurs. Liquid or powdered medicines can also be added to the dog's food, but don't be surprised if your dog takes one bite and refuses to touch the rest. If this is the case, powdered medicines can be liquefied by adding a little water; then proceed as above. Pills and capsules can be tricky, as dogs do not like them much and manage to trap them and spit them back out. The easiest way is to wrap the pill in something tasty—such as a small chunk of chopped meat, hot dog, or liverwurst—and hope that your pet will swallow it happily. If this fails, pry the dog's mouth open by applying gentle pressure near the canine teeth, tilt the head up slightly, and place the pill as far back on the tongue as possible. Close the dog's mouth and check for a swallow. Never hold a dog's head in an exaggerated upward position. This can cause the medicine to be inhaled into the windpipe.

Taking the Temperature

Knowing how to take the dog's temperature is very important. First of all, a dog's normal body temperature is slightly higher than a human's—approximately 100.5 to 102°F (38–38.9°C). To get the reading you will need a heavy-duty rectal thermometer that has been lubricated with a dab of petroleum jelly. It is best for two people to be present to avoid any chance of injury to the dog by preventing its thrashing about and breaking the thermometer. It is easiest to have the dog standing, but temperature can also be taken with the dog lying on its side. Have one person get a secure lock around the dog's chest while the other lifts the tail and inserts the thermometer. An accurate reading is available in two to three minutes. Electronic digital thermometers are moderately priced and yield rapid and accurate temperature readings. Labrador retrievers are generally fairly placid, so the second person is often not needed. Nevertheless, two people should be present the first few times to make sure the dog reacts favorably.

Taking the Pulse

It may become necessary to monitor your dog's heartbeat. The pulse is best obtained by pressing softly on the inside of the thigh, and can also be found on the front paw.
A normal heart rate is from 70 to 90 beats per minute, but may fluctuate due to such factors as age, stress, exertion, or disease. Your duty is to get the rate and record any unusual pattern of the beats if you notice any sudden change in your dog's condition, such as dizziness, fainting, or hyperactivity. Get the dog immediately to a veterinarian for a prompt diagnosis.

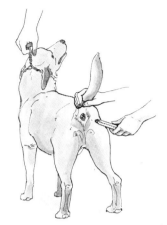

When taking your pet's temperature, have one person calm and secure the dog while the other lifts up the tail and gently inserts a heavy-duty rectal thermometer (lubricated with a little petroleum jelly) into the rectum.

Vaccinations

It is an owner's responsibility to see to it that a dog's health is properly protected from infectious diseases by getting it all necessary vaccinations. Veterinary science has perfected a number of vaccines that will make dogs immune to infectious diseases that are deadly to the unprotected, as evidenced by the epidemics that used to decimate dog populations before this protection was devised. Today these diseases can be eliminated if all owners do what is needed.

The breeder of your puppy should have begun this process by getting the litter its first set of vaccines (distemper, hepatitis, leptospirosis, parvovirus, and parainfluenza) at five to eight weeks of age. The new owner must carry this on by getting the pup the follow-up series of shots, on a schedule devised by your veterinarian. The dog will also need a rabies vaccine as well as booster shots of those vaccines that require follow-up treatment to retain immunity. Get a record of the initial

By making sure your dog's vaccinations are up-to-date, you will help ensure a long life. In most localities, you are required by law to have your dog vaccinated against rabies.

Given the proper attention, a Labrador retriever will be as healthy and well-adjusted as these dogs. Note the alert, inquisitive gaze and the bright eyes. The coats are sleek and shiny—the result of good grooming and good nutrition.

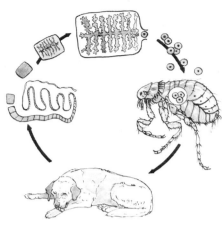

The life cycle of the dog tapeworm: Tapeworm eggs are ingested by fleas and hatch in the fleas' intestines. Should a dog ingest an infected flea, the tapeworms mature in the dog's intestines. Tapeworm eggs can also be ingested by eating uncooked meat or fish.

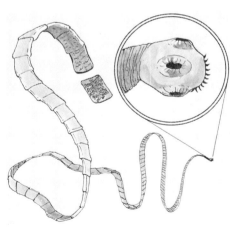

The dog tapeworm can range in length from less than an inch to more than a foot. The scolex, or head (see enlargement), must be killed and removed from the dog's system to cure a tapeworm infestation. The segments containing eggs are passed in the feces, thus providing a source of infection for other animals.

vaccinations from the pup's breeder for your and the veterinarian's records. At the initial checkup the puppy may also have been checked and treated for worms (which are very common in puppies), so be sure to find out if this was done, what type of worms were found, what the medication to cure the problem was, and how the dog reacted to the medicine.

Worms

Worms are common in dogs, especially puppies, but they should not be taken lightly. They should be cured only by a veterinarian who determines the proper dosage of the proper medicine for the specific type of worm involved. Cure-all home wormings by the inexperienced can be deadly. There is no need to routinely worm a dog. This should only be undertaken when the presence of worms is detected by microscopic evaluation of stool samples. Symptoms of worm infestation include a loss of appetite and/or weight, weakness, a bloated stomach, a lack of coat sheen, and diarrhea. Infested puppies may vomit up roundworms or pass them in their feces. Dogs of all ages may skid their anus along the ground, or scratch and bite at, or constantly lick the tail area to try to relieve the itch (see also Anal Glands). Some dogs show little of these outward signs until heavily infested, so have the tests for worms performed routinely (at least annually) even if your Labrador appears healthy.

The most common type of worm may be the roundworm, but cases of tapeworm and hookworm can also be found. Each requires its own medicine. Heartworm infestation, an often fatal disease spread by mosquitoes, used to be confined to the hot climates. Today it is almost everywhere. Heartworm is detected by a blood test, and if the dog is found to be free of this parasite, it is then placed on daily *preventative* medication. Once infected, a dog runs the risk of death, as heartworm is a very debilitating disease that is hard to cure. An annual blood test for this is a must.

As brief as this discussion may be, the long and short of it is that worms do exist, dogs must be routinely tested for their presence, and once discovered (hopefully not discovered, in the case of heartworm) they must be dealt with by a competent veterinarian. The owner's job is to keep an eye on the dog's overall condition, have the dog tested, and when necessary give the proper medication as specified by the veterinarian. That's enough. I cannot stress enough how dangerous it is to blindly worm a dog or puppy, as overdoses are very common and frequently fatal.

External Parasites

All dogs that frequent the outdoors will sooner or later come down with a case of flea infestation. In the summer, fleas are everywhere your Labrador wants to go, so be prepared to do battle against their presence on the dog and in your house. (While fleas seem to like all dogs, they also go for certain humans. My husband's ankles have proved to be especially vulnerable.) Fleas are nasty insects—they bite the host, itch like crazy, suck blood, and often pass on tapeworms. It takes a good effort to rid them from where they hide. Begin by purchasing a flea spray or powder from your veterinarian, pet shop, or grooming parlor. The dog's coat must be thoroughly doused with the repellent for it to work effectively, but be careful to apply it safely. Start at the head and work down the body, applying it against the grain of the coat. Take great care to protect and cover the dog's eyes, nose, and mouth, as such products can be very irritating to sensitive tissue. I would recommend two people doing the head: one to protect; one to

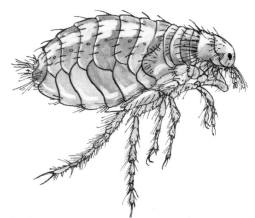

During warm weather you must protect your pet from fleas—which cause intense discomfort and transmit tapeworms.

slowly, carefully apply the anti-flea agent.

Anything frequently used by the dog (such as a crate or a bed) should also be sprayed to kill the breeding colonies not on the dog. If the fleas should work their way into the carpeting and furniture, apply a heavy-duty insect bomb (available in hardware stores) to the entire house and evacuate the area for several hours. There are also commercial products (sprays, powders, or liquids) that you can apply to your rug after the bombing to keep any embedded eggs from hatching and reinfesting the area.

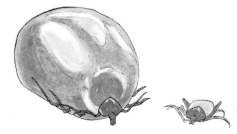

Ticks implant themselves in the skin and become enlarged as they suck the animal's blood.

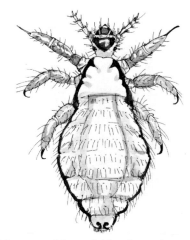

Lice cause intense itching. Inspect your Labrador's coat for clusters of eggs (called nits).

To help deter further infestations, place a flea collar on the dog when outside (you can remove it inside, if you like). Should the collar ever get wet, immediately remove it as it can be very irritating to the dog's skin. Should normal efforts fail to rid your dog of fleas, a flea dip should do the job. You can either take the dog to a professional groomer or carefully bathe the dog at home following the directions on the product.

Ticks are also common problems for Labradors, especially black ones whose dark coats mask their presence. Certain species are also the vectors of Lyme disease, which affects humans as well as other mammals. Ticks gnaw through the dog's skin and implant themselves in order to suck the dog's blood. They must be carefully removed, not simply ripped off, because improper removal can cause the head to be torn from the tick's body and remain imbedded in the dog's skin, where it may become infected or abscessed. To remove the tick, use tweezers or your thumb and first finger to grasp it as close to the skin as possible. Exert a firm but gentle constant upward pressure (don't twist, as this can tear the body). Some people prefer to apply tick dip (available from pet stores) to the site prior to removal. The dip suffocates the ticks and make the task easier. This is not necessary if care is taken to remove the tick properly. A thick, red spot may remain for several days where the tick was removed.

Caution: *Never* burn a tick off with a match or cigarette. This is simply dangerous and unnecessary.

There are several other types of external parasites that sometimes infest dogs, such as lice and mites, but these are less common (although equally serious). Both of these cause severe itching to the dog, are hard to get rid of, and can do great damage to the dog's coat. Routine inspection of the dog, especially during the hot summer months, should help keep any attacks under control by catching these problems in their early stages. Should you notice any small clusters of eggs or a rash of bumps or pustules on the dog's skin, take the dog to your veterinarian for an accurate diagnosis and appropriate treatment. Left unchecked, such disorders can be lifelong problems.

Insect Bites

Bee and insect stings are generally minor discomforts for a dog, and the owner is seldom aware that anything has happened. If you know that your dog has been bitten, check the site to see if the stinger is still imbedded. If it is, remove it with your fingernail by using a gentle scooping action at the base of the bite. Apply ice or wash the spot with cold water to reduce swelling and slow the flow of the venom.

Some dogs may develop a bump at the site or break out in a case of hives, which should clear without medical attention. Occasionally, however, a dog may have a severe allergic reaction to the bite and be put in a life-threatening situation. Shortly after being bitten, a hypersensitive dog will show a marked swelling and may have difficulty breathing. Your veterinarian should be consulted immediately.

My Tip: With most bites, some over-the-counter antihistamine or a corticosteroid will relieve most symptoms; ask your veterinarian before you apply any medication.

Common Disorders

Like humans, dogs are susceptible to a variety of mild, passing upsets. Unlike humans, they are unable to vocalize their complaints and give details of their symptoms. Consequently, it is up to the owner to keep a sharp eye on the dog's body language and make a decision about the seriousness of an illness.

Diarrhea

A mild case of diarrhea can have many causes: eating something indigestible, a change in diet, stress, a virus, etc. The first step in treatment is to withhold food for 12 to 24 hours to give the system a chance to clear itself out (water is permissible). A dose of Kaopectate or KaoCon will aid in reconditioning the intestines. If symptoms do not worsen over the 24-hour period, the dog can be given several small, bland meals the following day. The addition of a binding agent (such as rice or oatmeal) to the diet should be all that is needed.

Chronic diarrhea, diarrhea smeared with blood, or diarrhea accompanied by high fever and vomiting are danger signs that require veterinary assistance.

Vomiting

Vomiting can be associated with many illnesses affecting the digestive tract. As with diarrhea, most incidents of vomiting are quick to pass and are often due to the dog's having eaten something it shouldn't have. Left untreated, however, vomiting can quickly lead to dehydration and subsequent weight loss.

When the vomiting is limited to a few episodes, withhold the dog's food for 12 to 24 hours. If your veterinarian so advises, administer a small child's dose of Pepto-Bismol to help settle the stomach. If the vomiting does not recur (and there is no persistent fever or diarrhea), the dog may have several small meals during the next 24 hours. If all remains well, a normal diet may be resumed the following day. Should the condition persist, worsen, or should you notice any blood or worms in the vomit, a trip to the veterinarian is in order.

Some Labradors that gulp down their food are prone to vomiting shortly after eating (they usually re-eat the regurgitated food). While some dogs outgrow this pattern when they learn there is no frenzy needed to protect their meal from other predators, for others, it is a lifelong habit. If this is the case, it is best to feed the dog smaller amounts several times a day to avoid the problem.

Bloating

Large dogs, such as the Labrador retriever, are susceptible to bloating after drinking a large volume of water following a meal of dry kibble. The signs of bloating are abdominal distention, obvious distress, and unproductive attempts to vomit. This is a medical emergency for which you must seek immediate veterinary care.

Constipation

A change in diet is often the cause of mild constipation in dogs. Some dogs may also become constipated when confined for longer times than usual. In such cases, the addition of a little extra roughage in the food or administering a mild laxative such as Milk of Magnesia should cure the problem swiftly. If the condition lingers, your veterinarian may suggest the dog be given a glycerine suppository or a warm-water enema to relieve the blockage.

If the dog is actively straining, crying out in pain, and unable to pass any excrement, a serious health problem may exist. The dog may have a tumor in the intestines or may have swallowed an object that has lodged itself in the tract. Consult your veterinarian immediately.

Accidents: Cuts and Fractures

If your dog sustains a serious injury, you must act quickly to stabilize the situation and get the dog to professional help.

It is advisable that you acquaint yourself with common emergency procedures *before* they ever occur. A manual such as *First Aid for Your Dog* can provide you with lifesaving techniques. Your first act should be to calm and restrain the dog. This will prevent it from doing further damage to itself (there may be other injuries not apparent to you) and possibly injuring you. Even the mild-tempered Labrador may snap and bite when injured. Try to remain calm, and speak in low tones to the dog. Approach slowly. A thin piece of cloth, a stocking, a belt, or a tie can be used as a muzzle. Fold the material in half and place the center on the top of the muzzle. Cross the ends under the bottom of the jaw and bring them around to the back of the head, where you tie a secure knot (not too tight). You can now begin to assess the dog's needs. Do not move your pet unless absolutely necessary until you know the extent of the injury.

Locate the site of any bleeding and wash it gently with soap and warm water. If the blood continues to flow, apply pressure by placing a gauze pad or a clean cloth over the spot, wrapping another cloth securely around the limb

(if possible), and holding the compress in place. Any wound but a minor cut will require a veterinarian's attention, as it will have to be bandaged in a manner that inhibits the dog from removing it.

If the dog appears to have broken a bone, immobilize the animal as much as possible. Continued movement can result in damage to the muscles and nerves around the break site. Soothe the dog and get it to an emergency treatment facility as quickly as possible. A blanket can be used as a makeshift stretcher to transport the dog short distances.

If the dog is unconscious, check that its breathing passages are open. With the dog on its side, gently pry open its mouth and pull the tongue forward to allow air to flow. A dog can quickly go into shock, so keep it as calm as possible and cover it for added warmth.

Poisoning

This is an all-too-common occurrence, and most times you are unaware that your dog has ingested a poisonous substance. Symptoms are vomiting, diarrhea, lethargy, shaking, spasms, dizziness, cramps, and color change or bleeding in the mucous membranes. *Immediate* action is required.

If the source of the poisoning is obvious, you may be able to determine the first steps for treatment from the package. Specific antidotal information can often be obtained from the product label. Your veterinarian will need to know when and how much material the dog ingested to formulate a strategy for removing it from the body. Sometimes the poison can be neutralized in the stomach by specific antidotes, while in other cases the stomach may need to be pumped or the intestinal tract cleared. When little is known about what poison the dog has eaten, there is little chance of survival.

Common household items are the most notorious sources of poisoning in dogs (and children); keep such things as antifreeze, pesticides, cleaning agents, rat and mouse poisons, and painting supplies *locked up* to inhibit inquisitive investigation by your dog. Chocolate is another common item that must *never* be given dogs. In small doses, the result is diarrhea; in large doses, death is possible.

Anal Glands

At the bottom of the dog's anus are two glands, sometimes referred to as the "stink glands," that secrete a strong-smelling substance used as a scent marker by the dog. These glands are normally emptied by the defecation process, but they sometimes become impacted and need to be emptied manually. Symptoms of impacted anal glands are frequent licking of the area and/or dragging the anus along the floor or ground (see also Worms). If, upon inspection, the glands appear full, the fluid can be expressed by carefully pressing the outsides of the sac with your thumb and forefinger positioned at either side. The fluid should flow out and can be cleaned away.

Caution: Should the dog appear in discomfort when the sacs are touched, or if a pussy or bloody discharge is evident, the anal glands may be infected and will need treatment by your veterinarian.

Eye Diseases

Unfortunately, Labrador retrievers may inherit some eye defects that, in extreme cases, could lead to blindness. Progressive retinal atrophy (PRA) is a disease in which blindness develops gradually. Subtle changes in the appearance of the dog's retina are indicators. Retinal dysplasia causes poor eyesight, but rarely total blindness. This condition is not progressive. Juvenile cataracts are spots on the dog's lens that generally do not affect vision and are not progressive.

Any dog suspected of having an eye problem should be examined by a board certified veterinary ophthalmologist for diagnosis and treatment.

Epilepsy

Dogs with this affliction experience seizures. Although such incidents can also result from a variety of other conditions, such as infections, tumors, or trauma, epilepsy is thought to be a hereditary problem. It is usually treatable by medication from your veterinarian. Afflicted dogs should not be considered for breeding.

Hip Dysplasia

Hip dysplasia (HD) is a crippling congenital malformation that is caused when the ball of the thighbone does not fit properly into the socket of the hip joint, causing permanent damage to the joint. While severe cases may be evident in puppies showing an uneven gait, HD is generally a gradual, progressive disease that manifests itself at about one year of age. As an affected dog ages, movement becomes painful and the back legs become lame. While steps can be taken to relieve pain and slow the course of the disintegration of the joint by limiting exercise, there is no cure.

Because hip dysplasia is known to be hereditary, dogs should be X-rayed and evaluated for the condition when they are approximately one year old.

Ask your veterinarian to send the films to the Orthopedic Foundation for Animals (OFA) at the University of Missouri for evaluation. Dogs that pass the examination are issued a certificate.

Any dog exhibiting even a slight tendency toward this condition should not be considered for breeding. There is no future in producing dogs that cannot live up to their intended purpose. Through the efforts of dedicated breeders the progress of this condition can be thwarted, and hopefully eliminated in years to come.

Understanding the Labrador Retriever

The dog has succeeded in becoming our most treasured companion due to its adaptability. In the earliest times, the dog's ancestors—wolves, jackals, coyotes—learned to group together for survival, for hunting was easier in this manner. They developed pack behavior, whereby one animal assumed the leadership position and others fell in line behind, each working out its own niche in the line of power. This hierarchy is still found today in domesticated dogs.

As far back as 40,000 B.C. humans and doglike animals began to coexist. Through time, people and dogs formed mutually beneficial bonds. They became hunting partners and aided each other's survival. The dog became an ally and assistant to man, who assumed the leadership position. The dog adapted to the human pack.

Over the generations, humans devised new ways to cope with the environment. The dog soon learned to perform such tasks as herding the flocks and guarding against predators—both other people and animals. From these early beginnings the dogs of today take their form.

Many centuries have passed since dogs first joined forces with humans, and the early dogs have evolved into more than 140 distinct breeds, each with its own set of traits, characteristics, and instincts. To understand your Labrador retriever, you must understand its history as well as its heritage—an investigation that will require us to review the development of the breed over a period of approximately three centuries.

The 1800s to the Present

As with many breeds, the exact beginnings of the Labrador retriever cannot be pinpointed. Stories of coarse, thickly coated, black water dogs trained to work with fishermen date back to the sixteenth century, cited by sailors from Devon, England, who routinely saw them when trading with the fishermen of Newfoundland (then a British colony). Through the centuries more refined specimens emerged. These water dogs were known as Newfoundlands or Labrador Newfoundlands—titles that applied to several breeds of dogs found there. The dogs ranged from a large, heavy-coated variety known as the Large Newfoundland (progenitor of today's Newfoundland) to a smaller, rough-coated variety called the Lesser Newfoundland or St. John's Dogs. It is theorized that the modern-day Labrador retriever descends from the St. John's Dog, which was medium-sized, docile, easily managed, and possessed a very sensitive nose.

A number of breeds have been mentioned as early crosses that helped to set the type for the Labrador retriever. A likely pairing would be the St. John's with local black retrieving setters (then called water dogges). The resulting dogs likely featured a heavy, wavy coat. To evolve the hard, short coat that repelled the icy waters, crossings

This dog takes eagerly to the water on a retrieve. Its hard, short coat helps repel the water and keeps the dog warm.

A Labrador has a natural "soft mouth" that enables it to carry game without crushing it.

with black pointers or flat-coated retrievers may have taken place.

The Labrador retriever emerged as a distinct breed early in the nineteenth century and began to flourish as word of the breed's capabilities spread among sportsmen. This makes it a relatively new breed when compared with some of the hounds that can be traced back to several hundred years B.C.

The Labrador retriever may have called Newfoundland its homeland, but the breed was developed and refined in England. The name Labrador was finally settled on for the breed after its integration into the English sporting kennels in the 1800s. At this point basic breed structure and character were set and the breeding was kept pure. The continuous trade between England and Newfoundland meant an ample supply of Labradors could be imported for the earliest fanciers, who quickly recognized these dogs' superior talents for hunting and began breeding them in earnest for strictly private use. The breed was unknown as a companion dog for many generations, as Labradors were bred exclusively for work.

The earliest known breeders of Labradors were wealthy sportsmen who maintained large kennels of shooting dogs. The Fifth Duke of Buccleugh, the Tenth Earl of Home, and Lord John Scott were all very active in the 1840s. The most influential of the early breeders was the Third Earl of Malmesbury, who judiciously imported good specimens from the Newfoundland fishermen and is credited with having set the standard for quality Labrador retrievers. Many contemporary dogs can trace their pedigree to Malmesbury dogs, especially his renowned Tramp.

By the 1880s, word of this excellent worker had spread beyond the confines of the aristocracy's private kennels to sportsmen throughout England. However, two setbacks occurred that

threatened the breed's survival. In England, the Quarantine Act initiated a six-month quarantine for all imported livestock. In Newfoundland, the Sheep Protection Act of 1885 gave districts the right to prohibit dogs and to charge hefty fees for dog licensing, which resulted in many owners destroying all but those dogs needed to carry out their livelihood. Both actions severely limited the flow of new Labrador retrievers to England. Breeders were forced to work with the available stock and perfect the breed through careful selection. The conscientious efforts of these early breeders turned a potentially disastrous situation into a strengthening of the overall quality of the average Labrador retriever.

A. Holland Hibbert, later titled Third Viscount Knutsford, worked for more than 20 years to enhance breed type. Through his efforts the Labrador retriever was officially accepted into the English Kennel Club Stud Book in 1903, which led to the establishment of classes for Labradors at dog shows. Lord Knutsford's Munden Kennel achieved many "firsts": the first Labrador retrievers entered in the Stud Book were Knutsford's Sentry, Sovereign, and Single; the first Labrador to achieve a bench championship was his Broome Park Bob (1906); the first Labrador to place at a field trial was five-year-old Munden Single (1904); and the first field trial champion Labrador was Peter of Faskally, who descended from a Munden Labrador. A further descendant, Banchory Bolo, became the breed's first dual champion in 1922.

Through its sterling performance at field trials, the Labrador retriever was soon rivaling the flat-coated retriever for top spot among English sportsmen.

Labradors in America

In the 1920s the Labrador retriever began gaining a foothold with

American sportsmen. Although a few "English retrievers," as Labradors were called in nineteenth-century America, had made their way to our shores, few could be located in American shooting kennels prior to the 1920s, as setters and pointers were the dogs of choice in those days. In 1917, the first Labrador retriever registered by the American Kennel Club was imported from Scotland. Her name was Brocklehirst Floss.

The style of shooting in America at that time was different from that practiced abroad. A group of wealthy enthusiasts on the East coast with ties to Britain began developing the Labrador retriever among themselves in order to carry on the style of pass shooting to which they were most accustomed and partial. To aid in this, they not only imported fine dogs but also lured noted Scottish trainers to America. This was all the impetus the breed needed to become a force in the shooting game.

In 1931 the Labrador Retriever Club of America was founded and sponsored its first field trial in December of that year. The competition was held in Chester, New York, with a total of 16 entries—all but one of which were imports. The winner was Carl of Boghurst, a yellow owned by Mrs. Marshall Field. This annual event would spur popularity in the sport to the point where today there are more than 150 trials a year held for Labrador retrievers!

It was not until May 18, 1933, that the first specialty show for bench competition was held by the Labrador Club of America. From an entry of 34, Boli of Black was chosen as best. Boli, owned by Franklin P. Lord and purchased from the British breeder, Lady Howe, was the first American bench-champion Labrador retriever.

The Arden kennels of W. A. Harriman became the driving force in the field, claiming the first American field champion in Blind of Arden and the first female American field champion in Decoy of Arden—and they were littermates. Mr. Harriman's talent for beeding top-quality Labradors from his stock earned him the recognition of having developed the finest American kennel to date. His credits include four dual champions, five field champions, eight bench champions, and scores of champions that descend from this line. The shining star among the Arden Labradors was Shed of Arden, owned by Paul Bakewell. Shed was a dual champion who captured the National Championship competition three times in 1942 (the inaugural year), 1943, and 1946, a feat not equaled since. He embodied all that a Labrador should: talent in the field, beauty and intelligence, and the ability to produce quality offspring.

A mating of Mr. Harriman's Decoy with Dr. Milbank's Ch. Kaffles of Earlsmoor produced a litter from which Ch. Earlsmoor Moor of Arden emerged. Moor went on to win the Labrador Club of America Annual Specialty in 1938, 1939, 1940, 1941, and 1943. Winning a national specialty five times is an astounding accomplishment that may never be repeated again by *any* dog of *any* breed.

The postwar years were ones of great prosperity for the breed, yet demand for Labrador retrievers was such that it allowed for continued care and restraint to be used in the breeding programs throughout the country. While gaining a foothold in the American home as a companion pet, the Labrador retriever was still thriving as a true sporting dog and being bred primarily by knowledgeable owners.

In recent years the Labrador retriever has reached the pinnacle of its appeal, being among the top five of the most popular dogs in America. But unlike other breeds whose meteoric rise to the top has often led to indiscriminate breeding to mass-produce dogs to fulfill a faddish demand, the Labrador retriever has maintained and enhanced its quality in the postwar years. Today's Labrador retriever is a product of the fine early dogs and breeders who nurtured the breed through its infancy.

The Labrador Heritage: Working for People

As the breed name clearly points out, Labrador retrievers were bred originally to assist in the hunt by retrieving downed game. As years passed, their roles did not change but rather expanded to include numerous tasks and services.

Guide Dogs for the Blind

No service rendered by a dog can surpass the role of Guide Dog. Through the work of these highly skilled animals, a blind individual is able to move in the mainstream of life,

Labrador retrievers have the extraordinary intelligence, temperament, strength, and stamina needed to perform the task of Guide Dog for the blind.

guided by the "eyes at the end of the lead." Such a human-dog bond reaffirms the valued place canines have assumed in our modern world. Guide Dog and owner are a special pairing— a dog that lives to serve and an owner who is able to live life to its fullest aided by the service of a life-long companion and friend.

The Guide Dog program originated in Switzerland in the 1920s under the leadership of Mrs. Dorothy Eustis. The original Guide Dogs were strictly German shepherd females, bred by Mrs. Eustis at her Fonunate Field Kennels. Over the years, Labradors and golden retrievers were also recruited into the program. In Great Britain, approximately 70 percent of the Guide Dogs are Labrador retrievers, and Australia uses only Labradors for this task.

In the United States, The Seeing Eye was the driving force of the Guide Dog movement. This organization was begun in 1929 by Mrs. Eustis and is currently headquartered in Morristown, New Jersey. It has maintained its own breeding kennel since 1941, producing 327 puppies in 1986—117 of which were Labradors. Of a breeding stock of 40 adults, there are 15 Labrador bitches and four Labrador dogs. Only the very finest dogs are selected for this special breeding kennel. They must have successfully completed the rigorous training program designed by The Seeing Eye and exhibited stellar qualities in temperament and conformation. Labradors are commended as easy breeders producing large litters.

The Labrador retriever excels as a Guide Dog primarily because of its size, working ability, well-rounded temperament, and ability to get along so well with people. The Labrador also has a small streak of stubbornness that the people at The Seeing Eye find useful. While this makes the Labrador slightly tougher to train, this quality

This young yellow Labrador has been bred at the kennels of The Seeing Eye and will one day begin training for a life as a Guide Dog for the blind.

sets the breed apart from most in that a Labrador can take charge and refuse a command when confronted with an emergency situation—such as when a blind owner commands the dog to move forward and a hazard apparent only to the dog lies in the way.

Companion and Therapy Dogs

By far the most common use of today's Labrador is as the in-home companion—a "job" at which it excels. Surprisingly, the Labrador retriever was rarely kept *strictly* as a house pet until several decades after the breed's introduction to America. The initial fanciers of the breed became acquainted with it through knowledge of the shooting game. When the breed was well established as a sporting companion, its docile, brainy nature won its way out of the kennel and into the home. The Labrador retriever's ability to quickly adapt and respond to instruction made the transition quite easy. Today, puppies raised in the home actually become so entwined in the lives of their masters that they often suffer when relegated to the kennel life. (If you are planning to keep a kennel of Labradors, select puppies that are properly socialized but still familiar with kennel life.)

As a companion, the Labrador retriever is good-natured and gentle enough to accept the roughhousing of youngsters without returning it. If properly socialized while young, a Labrador will share its home with another dog, providing there is enough affection for all. It is more common for a Labrador to misbehave out of jealousy than out of dislike for another animal.

Labrador retrievers are long on self-control and loyalty, but they do not make the most avid watchdogs. As a rule, they are not overly suspicious of strangers or highly protective of loved ones, and when natural instincts are not stimulated they can

be inattentive to such a task. Always keen for a scent or sound, a Labrador retriever would certainly give voice at the approach of an intruder, but it might be won over by a friendly gesture or a luscious piece of sirloin. Left on sentry duty, a Labrador retriever may wander off in search of a scent that has caught its attention. In short, it is a people-dog. If you really need a watchdog, get your Labrador a German shepherd friend!

The value of companionship should not be underestimated. In recent years, obedience-trained Labradors as well as other breeds are being used as Therapy Dogs to enrich the lives of nursing home residents, aged shut-ins, and even emotionally disturbed children. The process is simple: a group of experienced dog handlers, such as those trained by Therapy Dogs International, bring their dogs to visit, perhaps put on an obedience performance for the audience, and then let animals and humans mingle, if conditions permit. The dogs are all obedience titlists who have proven themselves to be extremely gentle and outgoing. Their job is to make people feel wanted—and it works wonders for alleviating the loneliness and depression that often burden such lives. Labradors love people and the few hours Therapy Dogs share with others enrich both dog and man.

Military and Police Work

The Labrador's keen sense of smell and trainability have earned it a place in many police and military forces around the world. During World War II, Labradors were used throughout Europe to scout fields for undetected land mines. They were credited with many finds and exhibited a stick-to-it-iveness not found in other breeds tested for the job. They have also been trained as messengers to cover terrain that is all but impassable by man.

Many municipalities currently employ the services of skilled Labrador police dogs. They are primarily called upon for scent-discrimination details, such as tracking criminals in buildings or detecting hidden narcotics, weapons, and bombs. Once a substance has been detected, the dog does not retrieve the material unless specifically ordered by its master, but rather indicates the location to its trainer. This is to insure against possible injury to the dog.

Labradors can be found working in airports, on street patrol, and in other public locations, as it has been found that they have the concentration capacity and staying power to maintain scent work in large, populated areas. Labradors are becoming more popular in this job and have been touted for their ability to work among civilians without creating anxiety (which is often known to occur when the more traditional police dogs—German shepherds and Dobermans—are used).

Aiding the Handicapped

Having proved their love for humans and their desire to serve, Labradors are now being trained throughout the world to assist many types of handicapped owners in the chores of everyday life. With some assistance, many people who would formerly have been confined in their activities are now entering the mainstream of society. Their extensively trained Labradors are their vehicles to freedom.

As Labradors have extraordinary sense perceptions, they are one of the breeds being widely used as Hearing Ear Dogs. After completing a rigorous four- to six-month obedience and auditory awareness program, they are specifically trained to the individual needs of their hearing-impaired or deaf owners. Their primary tasks are to alert the owner to the noises that most people take for granted: the doorbell or telephone, the alarm clock, a baby crying, smoke alarms, oncoming traffic, or emergency sirens. The Hearing Ear Dog makes its master aware of any important sound by running between the sound and the owner until attention is paid, gently nudging a master who is asleep, or pulling the master from harm's way.

Aid Dogs are trained to assist physically disabled people with tasks requiring dexterity or mobility. These tasks run the gamut from picking up items dropped on the floor to bringing in the mail or turning light switches on and off. These skills are taught to a Labrador by building on its natural intelligence, retrieving instincts, gentle nature, and desire to please. After mastering a battery of advanced obedience techniques, each dog is placed with its disabled owner and taught the specific chores it will be required to perform in the home. With an arthritis sufferer, for example, the Aid Dog will retrieve or carry objects as commanded. With a more severely handicapped individual, such as a wheelchair-bound stroke victim or paraplegic, a system of communicating with the dog may also have to be devised to replace vocal commands or hand signals. Aid Dogs learn to assist their owners by performing many of the physical tasks they are unable to handle, in this way widening the owners' abilities to take an active role in the world around them.

Disaster Work

Following in the path of the legendary Saint Bernard, Labrador retrievers have become a vital part of rescue teams. Because of their keen sense of smell, Labradors are being trained to find people buried by the debris of earthquakes or similar disasters. The work is arduous and requires great concentration in dangerous

The Labrador retriever's hard, dense coat enables it to endure severe conditions while on rescue missions.

surroundings. The dog must go to its task in the rubble of collapsed buildings, surrounded by the clamor of emergency vehicles, and often fire.

The Labrador's superior scenting ability has made it one of the top Disaster Dogs because in these crisis situations the air is usually choked with dust, smoke, and gas escaping from broken gas lines. Labradors are able to focus on the human scent and locate trapped victims. Upon making a find, the Disaster Dog is trained to indicate this to its handler by barking and scratching gently at the spot. The intensity of the bark generally indicates whether the victim is dead or alive. The handler calls in another team to verify and then notifies the rescue officials, who do the removal.

Labrador retrievers work efficiently, in a calm, gentle manner, rather than the aggressive, almost attacking method exhibited by breeds that have been tried

but eliminated from the program. Each Disaster Dog has undergone extensive training and must be fully reliable to work individually off-lead and be totally responsive to its handler. Despite its desire to continue searching, a Disaster Dog must withdraw immediately upon command, as the handler may spot a danger that the dog is unaware of.

The Disaster Dog program is run by unpaid volunteers who teach the dogs to master all obedience skills as well as special techniques. A Disaster Dog must be trained to climb over difficult obstacles, such as ladders, thin walkways, rocks, and downed trees, and to avoid broken glass, collapsing surfaces, and other life-threatening situations. It must also be able to climb on its belly through small windows or crevices where people may be trapped. In short, such work requires a superlative dog dedicated to saving lives, putting its own on the line without fear.

Living with a Labrador

Although seldom uncontrollable or unruly, a Labrador is a lively animal with a great zest for life. Its natural curiosity and playfulness will inevitably lead it into various forms of "trouble." Until it is shown proper behavior by the owner, a Labrador believes the world is there for its personal pleasure. As mentioned, Labradors can be notorious chewers. During the various stages of teething, it is best to avoid mishaps by securing all treasured items and making a conscious effort to give the dog something permissible. Despite best efforts, few households containing a resident Labrador puppy will escape without at least one major "incident." In Jake's mind, not only did the glue on the spine of that nice dictionary taste good, but ripping out the pages and depositing them all over the house was fun. From time to time even a well-behaved adult will sneak an hors d'oeuvre from that low cocktail table when nobody is looking.

Labrador puppies will try to make toys and playthings out of items you would rather they leave alone—but who knows this until that first roll of toilet paper is stretched around several rooms or the potted plants are dug beyond recognition? The dog enjoys such actions and will continue to do so until caught in the act and corrected. Puppies are very much like children. Both make mistakes—sometimes unknowingly, sometimes willfully. Keep a wary eye on your Lab during its formative stages. Proper behavior is learned, not instinctive.

On the positive side, Labrador retrievers are very affectionate, loving dogs, and your little mischief maker will quickly work its way into your heart. Throughout life, it will prefer to be near you. Labradors are content to lie at your feet for hours, or be used as a child's television "pillow." They will often affectionately nuzzle your hand or face, and would prefer to go with you on any outing involving the car than be left behind. They can be counted on (when trained) to behave amicably and reliably with new faces, be they human or canine. Labradors have been known to sulk when excluded from family activities. Unlike many breeds, Labradors often share a powerful love for all the members of a household, not singling out or catering to one "favorite."

Labradors are loving, reliable companions for people of all ages. They are gentle and easy-going enough to withstand a moderate amount of teasing and roughhousing and make natural guardians for children. However, adults should always be present to supervise and make sure that the play does not get too vigorous for the children or dog.

The Labrador Identity

As highly refined as today's Labrador retriever may be, it still retains its pack instinct. It functions best as an established member of a group, with each member of its "pack" (household) assuming a certain rank according to their leadership position. Given an opening, a dog will assert itself and vie for the leadership role. This basic pack concept is at the heart of the human-dog relationship. Once humans have assumed their rightful leadership positions, the dog can learn its place and enjoy its role as companion, not leader. Learning to understand a dog's basic instincts and how to communicate effectively are immensely important tasks. Some of the trials and tribulations of puppyhood can perhaps be avoided, or at least understood, by remembering that a dog will try to assert its leadership potential while young. An owner must set the dog straight from the beginning, or suffer the consequences. I am not saying that an owner must try to break the dog's spirit in order to get along. On the contrary, it is the lively spirit of the Labrador retriever that is so appealing. A successful owner must be a consistent, guiding force in the dog's life—the undisputed leader, the "alpha." This will then foster a sense of loyalty and self-confidence in the dog, as it can adjust to its role and feel comfortable with it.

During the first eight weeks of a puppy's life, its dam was the alpha figure. She was the dominant force in the litter's life and instilled in them a basic sense of discipline. When separated from its dam, the puppy will take its shot at the alpha spot. A wise owner will understand this adolescent ploy and firmly, yet fairly, take charge.

Remember: To help mold your Labrador retriever into a well-adjusted adult, there are some basic concepts to bear in mind. A dog responds to its master according to its interpretation of that person's vocal tone and body language. Take a lesson from this and learn to read and understand what your dog's postures, vocalizations, and facial expressions are telling you.

Posture, Facial Expression, and Vocalization

Canine body language is basically uniform among all breeds of dogs. A Labrador will instinctively know what the stance of the Great Dane next door is communicating, as well as the struts of the local beagle. While anyone can easily tell the difference between a friendly greeting bark and a warning growl, by paying attention to your dog and its moods you will learn to recognize the difference and significance of the various pitched whines, moans, and barks that a dog produces. Reading the accompanying body language is the key.

When at ease, the Labrador's body will appear relaxed; the head and ears are up, and the tail is at rest. When at attention, the ears will point forward more, the tail will be held horizontal, and the dog will look more up on its toes. When happy, as in greeting a familiar person, the tail will move swiftly on a horizontal line and the dog may do some whining (if not taught otherwise, it may also try to jump and lick your lips, being a very affectionate breed). Labradors are often known to "smile" when happy, as their lips draw tight and back, exposing their teeth. In some breeds this response is often misinterpreted as a snarl, but with the Labrador this expression is generally quite comical, leaving little doubt that the dog is glad to see you.

Submissive posture is often mistaken as the dog's "guilty" look. This is incorrect. A submissive posture is typified by the dog lowering itself near the ground, tail down or tucked under its belly. The ears point back, and the dog will avoid direct eye contact. In groveling fashion, it will try to lick the mouth or hands of the dominant person (or dog). The dog may roll onto its back, and may even urinate as a sign of further submission.

When confused or upset, the dog may also assume a lowered stance but will rapidly pant rather than try to lick. Neither of these postures should be associated with our notion of guilt. They are reactions to the authority of a more dominant being and often signs of stress in the animal. When exhibiting these behaviors, the animal is incapable of learning, as self-confidence is low.

Caution: An aggressive, offensive posture (one you will rarely see with a Labrador) is one where the head, body, tail, and even the hair along the spine are all very much upright. The facial expression is obviously one of anger, with exposed teeth, and the dog emits a low, warning growl. It appears as if it will attack. Conversely, should a dog feel threatened, it assumes a lowered, defensive position, ears back, with the tail down and under. The facial expression is again harsh (this time from fear), with teeth exposed, and there is a low growling.

Communication

A good example of miscommunication between owner and pet is this familiar scenario: An owner comes into a room and finds an unwanted "deposit" on the rug, screeches in anger, and admonishes the dog, which is by now crouched low to the floor, scurrying to the safety of the farthest corner. The owner thinks the dog knows it has done wrong. On the contrary; the dog hears loud tones, sees anger on its master's face, tries to get away, and assumes a submissive posture as an act of self-preservation. It has not been given any rea-

Labradors are the type of companion that children love to share secrets with.

son to associate its actions with the master's reactions, and the whole episode is counterproductive to learning and bonding.

Labradors learn from positive experiences. In theory, the process is quite simple: You clearly let the dog know what you want it to do, the dog does it, you lavish the dog with praise, repeat the entire process several times, and it learns. The reality is that each dog and each teacher are individuals with their own strengths and weaknesses. Some Labradors learn quickly, others need encouragement and numerous repetitions. Sometimes a dog just cannot comprehend a certain command and a new technique for teaching that action must be developed. A balance must be struck.

Be alert and realize what your tone and body and facial expressions are telling your dog, and what your dog's body language is telling you. By analyzing the dog's actions and reactions, you should be able to figure out what further steps may be needed ("Jake is testing me, I need to reinforce who's boss"; "Jake is confused, I need to show him what I expect of him"; "Jake is chewing shoes again—I need to find out why and show him that misbehavior will not be tolerated").

With proper training, Labrador retrievers make excellent hunting companions. They are content enough to wait in the field for their chance to retrieve fowl or other game. When called upon, they take eagerly to the water, whatever the conditions. They have a naturally "soft mouth" that enables them to deliver game without marring it in any way.

The Quality Labrador

Whether your Labrador retriever is destined to be a show competitor, a hunting partner, or a companion in the home—and the breed excels at all three aspects—a general knowledge of the working heritage of the Labrador should clarify what a quality specimen is and why this is important to all owners.

The Labrador retriever was developed by sportsmen to work in the field and retrieve game. Luckily the breed evolved quite naturally, with improvements being made by educated selection from within the breed itself, rather than the "quick fix" of an outcross to a breed with desirable qualities. This has yielded an overall steadiness to the inheritance patterns of the Labrador's temperament and structure (called conformation). Such steadiness enhances the quality of the *average* specimen, which means that with rare exception today's typical Labrador retriever will be able to perform the

In competition at dog shows the Labrador will be thoroughly examined by the judges to determine its compliance with the points of the breed standard.

task it was originally bred for, whether ever asked to do this or not. While outstanding dogs may win recognition for themselves and their breeders (and rightfully so!), such standouts are few. The overall quality of the average specimen is the best indicator of the condition of a breed.

A quality Labrador should be endowed with an instinct for the retrieve and a conformation that allows the dog to fulfill its working potential effortlessly. Such work requires a strong dog with staying power. The Labrador retriever must be able to work long and hard—running in overgrown terrain, swimming in turbulent waters, carrying a downed bird for long distances. The compact, well-balanced body of the Labrador enables it to fulfill its purpose by design.

The following is the official breed standard as prepared by the Labrador Retriever Club and approved by the American Kennel Club. A standard is the verbal depiction of the perfect specimen of the breed. Few dogs come close to fulfilling all the exacting specifications of a standard, but it serves as the guideline for conformation evaluation and for breeders to follow when evaluating which dogs should be used in breeding programs. The standard describes not only the quality Labrador but the *ideal* Labrador. See page 65 for an illustration showing the major points of the Labrador retriever's anatomy.

The Labrador Retriever Club revised its breed standard in 1994 for the first time in more than 30 years. The new standard that follows offers breeders and fanciers a much more in-depth guideline for assessing their Labrador. Included in the new standard are five disqualifications that were not previously contained in the breed standard. These oversee proper height, nose and eye pigment, tail docking, and color.

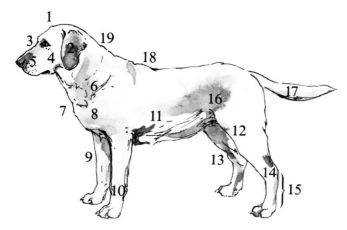

Parts of the Labrador

1. Skull
2. Ear
3. Stop
4. Cheek
5. Muzzle
6. Shoulder
7. Chest
8. Brisket
9. Forequarters
10. Front Pastern
11. Ribcage
12. Stifle
13. Hindquarters
14. Hock
15. Rear Pastern
16. Loin
17. "Otter" Tail
18. Withers
19. Neckline

To receive top honors, a show-quality Labrador will have to exhibit the points specifically detailed in the breed standard and display an eager, outgoing personality.

AKC Labrador Retriever Standard

General Appearance

The Labrador retriever is a strongly built, medium-sized, short-coupled dog possessing a sound, athletic, well-balanced conformation that enables it to function as a retrieving gun dog; the substance and soundness to hunt waterfowl or upland game for long hours under difficult conditions; the character and quality to win in the show ring; and the temperament to be a family companion. Physical features and mental characteristics should denote a dog bred to perform as an efficient retriever of game with a stable temperament suitable for a variety of pursuits beyond the hunting environment.

The most distinguishing characteristics of the Labrador retriever are its short, dense, weather-resistant coat; an "otter" tail; a clean-cut head with broad back-skull and moderate stop; powerful jaws; and it's "kind," friendly eyes, expressing character, intelligence, and good temperament.

Above all, a Labrador retriever must be well-balanced, enabling it to move in the show ring or work in the field with little or no effort. The typical Labrador possesses style and quality without overrefinement, and substance without lumber or cloddiness. The Labrador is bred primarily as a working gun dog; structure and soundness are of great importance.

Size, Proportion and Substance

Size: The height at the withers for a dog is 22½ to 24½ inches (57.2–62.2 cm); for a bitch is 21½ to 23½ inches (54.6–54.7 cm). Any variance greater than ½ inch (1.3 cm) above or below

The Labrador's skull is fairly wide, with a slightly pronounced brow.

these heights is a disqualification. Approximate weight of dogs and bitches in working condition: dogs 65 to 80 pounds (29.5–36.3 kg); bitches 55 to 70 pounds (24.9–31.8 kg).

The minimum height ranges set above shall not apply to dogs or bitches under twelve months of age.

Proportion: Short-coupled; length from the point of the shoulder to the point of the rump is equal to or slightly longer than the distance from the withers to the ground. Distance from the elbow to the ground should be equal to one half of the height at the withers. The brisket should extend to the elbows, but not perceptibly deeper. The body must be of sufficient length to permit a straight, free, and efficient stride; but the dog should never appear low and long or tall and leggy in outline.

Substance: Substance and bone proportionate to the overall dog. Light, "weedy" individuals are definitely incorrect; equally objectionable are cloddy, lumbering specimens. Labrador retrievers shall be shown in working condition well-muscled and without excess fat.

Head

Skull: The skull should be wide; well developed but without exaggeration. The skull and foreface should be on parallel planes and of approximately equal length. There should be a moder-

ate stop—the brow slightly pronounced so that the skull is not absolutely in a straight line with the nose. The brow ridges aid in defining the stop. The head should be clean-cut and free from fleshy cheeks; the bony structure of the skull chiseled beneath the eye with no prominence in the cheek. The skull may show some median line; the occipital bone is not conspicuous in mature dogs. Lips should not be square off or pendulous, but fall away in a curve toward the throat. A wedge-shaped head, or a head long and narrow in muzzle and back skull, is incorrect as are massive, cheeky heads. The jaws are powerful and free from snippiness—the muzzle neither long and narrow nor short and stubby.

Nose: The nose should be wide and the nostrils well developed. The nose should be black on black and yellow dogs, and brown on chocolates. Nose color fading to a lighter shade is not a fault. A thoroughly pink nose or one lacking in any pigment is a disqualification.

Teeth: The teeth should be strong and regular with a scissors bite; the lower teeth just behind, but touching the inner side of the upper incisors. A level bite is acceptable, but not desirable. Undershot, overshot, or misaligned teeth are serious faults. Full dentition is preferred. Missing molars or premolars are serious faults.

Ears: The ears should hang moderately close to the head, set rather far back, and somewhat low on the skull; slightly above eye level. Ears should not be large and heavy, but in proportion with the skull, and reach to the inside of the eye when pulled forward.

Eyes: Kind, friendly eyes imparting good temperament, intelligence, and alertness are a hallmark of the breed. They should be of medium size, set well apart, and neither protruding nor deep set. Eye color should be brown in black and yellow Labradors, and brown

The musculature of the Labrador reveals the powerful build of this strong breed.

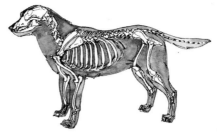

The skeleton of the Labrador retriever. The chest is deep and the legs are of medium length.

or hazel in chocolates. Black or yellow eyes give a harsh expression and are undesirable. Small eyes set close together or round prominent eyes are not typical of the breed. Eye rims are black in black and yellow Labradors; and brown in chocolates. Eye rims without pigmentation is a disqualification.

Neck, Topline, and Body

Neck: The neck should be of proper length to allow the dog to retrieve game easily. It should be muscular and free from throatiness. The neck should rise strongly from the shoulders with a moderate arch. A short, thick neck or a "ewe" neck is incorrect.

Topline: The back is strong and the topline is level from the withers to the croup when standing or moving. However, the loin should show evidence of flexibility for athletic endeavor.

Body: The Labrador should be sort-coupled, with good spring of ribs tapering to a moderately wide chest. The Labrador should not be narrow chested; giving the appearance of hollowness between the front legs, nor should it have a wide spreading, bulldog-like front. Correct chest conformation will result in tapering between the front legs that allows unrestricted forelimb movement. Chest breadth that is either too wide or too narrow for effi-

The Labrador in motion exhibits a well-muscled physique. Movement is free and effortless, giving the appearance of power and strength.

67

cient movement and stamina is incorrect. Slab-sided individuals are not typical of the breed; equally objectionable are rotund or barrel-chested specimens. The underline is almost straight, with little or no tuck-up in mature animals. Loins should be short, wide, and strong; extending to well-developed, powerful hindquarters. When viewed from the side, the Labrador retriever shows a well-developed, but not exaggerated forechest.

Tail: The tail is a distinguishing feature of the breed. It should be very thick at the base, gradually tapering toward the tip, of medium length, and extending no longer than to the hock. The tail should be free from feathering and clothed thickly all around with the Labrador's short, dense coat, thus having that peculiar rounded appearance that has been described as the "otter" tail. The tail should follow the topline in repose or when in motion. It may be carried gaily, but should not curl over the back. Extremely short tails or long thin tails are serious faults. The tail completes the balance of the Labrador by giving it a flowing line from the top of the head to the tip of the tail. Docking or otherwise altering the length or natural carriage of the tail is a disqualification.

Forequarters

Forequarters should be muscular, well coordinated, and balanced with the hindquarters.

Shoulders: The shoulders are well laid-back, long, and sloping; forming an angle with the upper arm of approximately 90 degrees that permits the dog to move its forelegs in an easy manner with strong forward reach. Ideally, the length of the shoulder blade should equal the length of the upper arm. Straight shoulder blades, short upper arms or heavily muscled or loaded shoulders, all restricting free movement, are incorrect.

Front Legs: When viewed from the front, the legs should be straight with good strong bone. Too much bone is as undesirable as too little bone, and short-legged, heavy-boned individuals are not typical of the breed. Viewed from the side, the elbows should be directly under the withers, and the front legs should be perpendicular to the ground and well under the body. The elbows should be close to the ribs without looseness. Tied-in elbows or being "out at the elbows" interfere with free movement and are serious faults. Pasterns should be strong and short and should slope slightly from the perpendicular line of the leg. Feet are strong and compact, with well-arched toes and well-developed pads. Dewclaws may be removed. Splayed feet, hare feet, knuckling over, or feet turning in or out are serious faults.

Hindquarters

The Labrador's hindquarters are broad, muscular, and well developed from the hip to the hock with well-turned stifles and strong, short hocks. Viewed from the rear, the hind legs are straight and parallel. Viewed from the side, the angulation of the rear legs is in balance with the front. The hind legs are strongly boned, muscled with moderate angulation at the stifle, and powerful, clearly defined thighs. The stifle is strong and there is no slippage of the patellae while in motion or when standing. The hock joints are strong, well let down and do not slip or hyperextend while in motion or when standing. Angulation of both stifle and hock joint is such as to achieve the optimal balance of drive and traction. When standing, the rear toes are only slightly behind the point of the rump. Overangulation produces a sloping topline not typical of the breed. Feet are strong and compact, with well-arched toes and well-developed pads. Cowhocks, spread hocks, sickle hocks, and overangulation are serious structural defects and are to be faulted.

Coat

The coat is a distinctive feature of the Labrador retriever. It should be short, straight, and very dense, giving a fairly hard feeling to the hand. The Labrador should have a soft, weather-resistant undercoat that provides protection from water, cold, and all types of ground cover. A slight wave down the back is permissible. Woolly coats, soft silky coats, and sparse slick coats are not typical of the breed, and should be severely penalized.

Color

The Labrador retriever coat colors are black, yellow, and chocolate. Any other color or a combination of colors is a disqualification. A small white spot on the chest is permissible, but not desirable. White hairs from aging or scarring are not to be misinterpreted as brindling.

Blacks: Blacks are all black. A black with brindle markings or a black with tan markings is a disqualification.

Yellows: Yellows may range in color from fox-red to light cream; with variations in shading on the ears, back, and underparts of the dog.

Chocolates: Chocolates can vary in shade from light to dark chocolate. Chocolate with brindle or tan markings is a disqualification.

Movement

Movement of the Labrador retriever should be free and effortless. When watching a dog move toward oneself, there should be no sign of elbows out. Rather, the elbows should be held neatly to the body with the legs not too close together. Moving straight forward without pacing or weaving, the legs should form straight lines, with all parts moving in the same plane. Upon viewing the dog from the rear, one should have the impression that the hind legs move as nearly as possible in a parallel line with the front legs. The hocks should do their full share of the work, flexing well, giving the appearance of power and strength. When viewed from the side, the shoulders should move freely and effortlessly, and the foreleg should reach forward close to the ground with extension. A short, choppy movement or high knee action indicates a straight shoulder; paddling indicates long, weak pasterns; and a short, stilted rear gait indicates a straight rear assembly. All are serious faults. Movement faults interfering with performance, including weaving; side-winding; crossing over; high knee action; paddling; and short, choppy movement, should be severely penalized.

Temperament

True Labrador retriever temperament is as much a hallmark of the breed as the "otter" tail. The ideal disposition is one of a kindly, outgoing, tractable nature; eager to please and nonaggressive toward man or animal. The Labrador has much that appeals to people; its gentle ways, intelligence, and adaptability make it an ideal dog. Aggressiveness toward humans or other animals or any evidence of shyness in an adult should be severely penalized.

Disqualifications

1. Any deviation from the height prescribed in the standard.
2. A thoroughly pink nose or one lacking in any pigment.
3. Eye rims without pigment.
4. Docking or otherwise altering the length or natural carriage of the tail.
5. Any other color or a combination of colors other than black, yellow, or chocolate as described in the standard.

Though the Labrador has inherited both a natural desire and an ability for retrieving, each dog must be trained in proper procedure. The dog must be taught to wait on the alert for not only the throw but for the command to fetch the object. Once released, the dog should head directly to the object and return it to the trainer. The trainer will instruct the dog on where to place the object once the retrieve is completed.

Training Your Labrador

Training your Labrador retriever to be a mannerly adult is begun at birth, by its mother. Once the puppy arrives at the new owner's home, it has already been given some basic instructions on behavior—so don't be fooled into thinking it is too young to behave. A puppy is, of course, too young to teach formal commands, but early lessons in manners and on who is in charge can begin at once.

The Labrador retriever is a highly intelligent animal and a capable learner. It embodies many natural instincts and abilities that make this breed distinct among others of similar heritage. But at the core, a Labrador retriever is a dog—originally a pack animal. From earliest times, pack animals have exhibited a pattern of behavior that affects the process of training: A pack animal assumes it is the boss until proved otherwise (the leader-of-the-pack syndrome). At birth, the dam assumes the leadership position and keeps her young in line. As the puppies begin to assert their independence, she will remind them of their place through low growls, a swat of the paw, or an occasional shake of the neck. Little else is necessary. She admonishes her young swiftly, fairly, consistently, and unemotionally, and they respect her position as leader. The wise owner follows the dam's example.

Consistency is vital. Should the dog misbehave, respond accordingly and appropriately. Do not let Jake's "cute little antics" go uncorrected as this will undermine your leadership. Respond firmly but fairly, letting him know what is expected of him and what will not

be tolerated. Brute force is not required and is counterproductive. When a dog is testing your authority, correct it in a manner a dog will understand—a firm vocal reprimand, a stern look, a shake of the neck. Little more should be necessary to make your displeasure clear if you are carrying out the corrections authoritatively. Be sure never to whine, nag, plead, or preach at the dog, as these are clearly not the actions of a leader and the dog will not feel compelled to obey.

With this guideline for the psychology of discipline in mind, we can now proceed to some beginning training lessons.

Training the Puppy: Some Early Successes

Labrador retriever owners are blessed with a breed that loves to learn. All training must enforce the idea that learning not only is fun but it will bring positive responses from the owner. Learning is not a game, but it need not be unpleasant either.

The earliest training is quite simple: Get Jake to respond to his name and praise him. This is, of course, easily accomplished by simply using his name whenever dealing with the dog. Responding when addressed gives the dog its first success. It discovers that a correct response brings rewards, and Labradors thrive on such positive reinforcement. The dog bonds to you and learns to want to please you.

The housetraining process is the puppy's first real challenge (see details of the housebreaking process in Chapter 2, "Basic Rules of Labrador

Care," page 18). If handled properly, this should not be a battle and should be accomplished quickly. Through successes the dog learns confidence—both in itself and in you, the leader. The dog learns that you respond positively when it reacts in a certain manner to certain situations. When the dog acts otherwise, it is corrected. This praise/correction pattern lays the foundation for learning and must be constant. Mistakes will be made, but, with guidelines, the dog learns what it can and cannot do. Formal training is simply teaching the dog that certain actions require a certain reaction.

Lessons: Rules to Train By

Common sense should be your guide in deciding when to begin formal training. It is useless and frustrating for all involved to begin training a puppy that cannot understand what you want of it. As a general rule, most Labradors can begin command training at six to eight months of age. Concentration is the key. If the puppy constantly wanders off—physically or mentally—it is probably too young.

Lessons should be short at first, no more than ten minutes, but they should be held regularly. Twice daily is the schedule of preference. Repeat all lessons frequently, but not to a point where the dog can no longer concentrate or where it shows no interest. Boredom can do serious damage to a training program.

Keep the atmosphere serious, but not tedious. You do not want the puppy to think training is all great fun, but it should not be drudgery either. Praise the dog for each minor success, but don't go overboard with your approval and reduce the dog to a quivering mass of joy at your feet.

Commands should be firm and authoritative, but not scolding. Be sure to issue the same command each time you request a certain action (not "Jake, come" one time and "Come here, boy" the next). As a general rule, you should include the dog's name in a command requiring motion (heel, come) but omit it from the commands where the dog is to remain motionless (sit, stay, down).

Verbal corrections are instantaneous: "No!" You then repeat the command and show the proper response. Repeat the command only when absolutely needed, as your goal is to have the dog perform the correct response with *only one command.*

Progress *slowly,* as an action quickly learned is often quickly forgotten. Be patient, as many repetitions of an action will be needed to truly impress upon the dog the knowledge of how it is to respond.

Remember: Correct fairly and with love, not out of anger. The dog is probably making mistakes out of confusion, not willful misbehavior. Never shout or strike the dog, as this will only make matters worse. Emphasize the dog's successes rather than harp on its mistakes.

By keeping the lessons short and pleasant, you will keep the dog interested in learning more. Do not push the dog beyond its capabilities, even if things are going well. Pushing for "just one more" can lead to exhaustion and disinterest.

Follow the lesson with a pleasant activity, such as a walk or a game. The dog will appreciate the special attention and regard training as pleasurable.

The early training your dog receives will affect it the rest of its life. To become a beloved companion in the home, the dog must learn how to behave in a variety of circumstances. To accomplish this, both owner and dog must make a concerted effort to master all the basic commands.

HOW-TO:
Collar and Lead

Introducing the Collar

The collar and lead are the primary tools of training. You may want to familiarize the young puppy with the feel of a collar by having it wear a light-weight collar when young, but no collar is really necessary until formal training is to begin. When the puppy shows that it is able to concentrate on the sound of your voice, you can turn your play into training. You will need a training or "choke" collar, which consists of a chain of metal links with a ring on each end. This collar should only be worn during teaching sessions. The training collar allows you to apply as much pressure as necessary to evoke the correct response or action by the dog. A light snap upwards is all that is needed to get the dog's attention and alert

Chain choke collars (top) are for use when training. For general wear a good-fitting leather or nylon collar (bottom) can be used to attach identification tags and licenses .

To form the choke collar, slip the chain through one of the rings and attach the leash to the free (top) ring.

it to correct its misdeed. The collar will momentarily tighten. Once the pressure is released, it will immediately loosen. The dog will quickly learn that the upward tug and the resultant tightening signify displeasure and that a correction is needed.

Used properly the training collar is a valuable teaching aid. It should *never* be used inhumanely to inflict pain.

Always choose a size that is appropriate for the dog—approximately the diameter of the head plus one to two inches. Overly large collars can be dangerous and are useless for quick corrections, so don't buy one the puppy will "grow into."

To form the training collar, slip the chain through one of the rings. The lead will attach to the free ring. When placing the collar on the dog's neck, be sure to slip it over the head so that the chain connecting to the free ring passes *over the top* of the neck,

not under. This positioning will allow the collar to relax instantly once the upward pressure is released. The rings should be positioned on the right side of the dog's neck, as the dog will always stand to your left during the training process.

The Harness

Once your Labrador has adjusted to the primary collar and lead, you may want to introduce the use of the harness. The harness fits over the dog's back and chest, going through the legs. The lead is attached along a strap on the back. When using the harness, there is no pull on the neck of the dog. Many owners prefer the harness for dogs that require little correction. It is also a good tool to use on a dog that surges ahead and tugs on the lead. The correction available from the harness gives the

Spring clips for dog's leashes (left to right): a clip with a safety catch, a scissors-type clip, and a simple spring clip.

Walking Your Puppy

Once your Lab has adapted to the feel of the lead, pick the lead up but apply no pressure. Walk around with the puppy for several minutes, following wherever it wanders. Make this a fun exercise. Now let the pup know it is time to follow you. Slowly introduce the feel of the upward tug. If it is frightened, reassure it but continue to apply firm pressure whenever it wanders out of your control area. In a short time you should be able to impress on the puppy that the lead is a restraint that must be obeyed and that the gentle tugs demand immediate attention. The dog will soon be walking according to your guidance. At this point, formal command instruction can begin.

A harness is a great way to help your dog become more comfortable on the lead. Unlike the choke collar, the harness puts little pressure on the neck. Many dogs find this type of restraint easier to accept.

owner good control over the forward motion of the dog.

Once you have placed the collar on the dog's neck, offer praise and let the dog wear it for a day. For safety's sake, you may want to attach a small metal medallion to the dog's collar listing the dog owner's name, address, and phone number and any health problems the dog may have. These name tags are available at most pet stores and can be invaluable in times of medical emergencies or when a dog gets lost.

Introducing the Lead

When the dog no longer balks at the feel of the collar, attach a lead. The training lead is 6 feet (1.8 m) long, ½ to 1 inch (1.3–2.5 cm) in width, and generally made of a light but sturdy webbed cloth, nylon, or leather. Correct with "No!" if your dog tries to chew the lead. The lead is a

symbol of authority, not a toy, so be firm. If necessary, apply a slight upward tug to remove it from the dog's grasp. At first you can let the puppy drag the lead around with it to accustom it to this sudden weight, but monitor the situation closely in case it becomes frightened and to make sure it does not get tangled and possibly hurt.

The reel lead is an efficient means of controlling the amount of freedom you allow your dog when strolling.

Be sure to reinforce the basics: the dog must sit by your side and await a further command.

When the command is given, the dog should respond without hesitation.

The dog must not lunge ahead when learning to heel.

The stay requires great self-control, so reward each attempt with lots of praise and affection.

The Basic Commands

Whether your Labrador will be a hunting companion, a house pet, or a show or field-trial competitor, it must learn the five basic commands: sit, heel, stay, come, and down. Knowledge of these commands means the dog can be trusted to participate in activities with humans. Until trustworthy, the dog should be kept on lead, tethered, or secluded away from activities where self-control is necessary. This is not punishment—this is restraint. Participation should be the dog's reward for learning proper behavior and self-restraint. The responsibility of teaching your Labrador retriever the basic requirements lies with you, the owner. Labradors are, by nature, willing and avid learners. Your task is to teach your dog to obey you instantly, with only one command. Accept no less, as your Labrador retriever is a capable learner.

Sit

The "sit" is taught with the dog on lead, preferably indoors in an area free from distractions. The dog should be taught first to sit at your left side, with its shoulders square to your knee. Once it has mastered this position, it can later be taught the sit in front. Begin by placing the dog at your side, with the lead in your right hand. Keep the lead taut, applying a slight amount of upward pressure to help keep the dog's head up. Command "Sit" while you firmly press your left hand on its rear and place it in the sitting position. Continue the upward pressure from the lead in your right hand and use your left to straighten. Offer praise as soon as the dog is properly positioned, and release it with "Good boy !" or an upward sweep of your left hand. Make the initial attempts quite short, thus not allowing the dog the opportunity to fall over on your leg or lie down. Gradually increase the sit time; be sure to praise

To get your Labrador to sit, maintain an upward pressure on the leash with your right hand as you command the dog to "sit" and push firmly on its rear with your left hand.

the dog when it reaches the sit position, not as it sits or when it breaks to get up. It must learn to associate the praise with the action. Should the dog attempt to move out of position, correct with "No!" and a slight jerk from the lead.

As the dog progresses, the pressure on the rear should be reduced and finally removed, as the sitting action becomes habitual in response to the command. At this point you can build on this knowledge and begin training two further commands: "heel" and "stay."

Heel

Heeling is no more than a controlled walking—an act every dog should be expected to perform. The dog is always to be on your left side, its chest preferably in line with your knee. The lead is held by your right hand and corrective pressure is applied by your left. Place the dog in a sit. Begin by stepping off with your left foot, calling "Jake, heel!" as you move forward. Snap the leash as you give the command to start him forward, removing the pressure as he responds. Walk at a comfortable pace, applying pressure

When teaching the "heel," hold the bulk of the leash in your right hand. Should the dog try to move away from your side, apply upward pressure with your left hand.

only if he surges ahead or lags behind. Make your snaps firm and repeat "Heel!" with each correction. Praise him as soon as he responds, using a pleasant tone and "Good boy!" Repeat the praise—but do not overdo it—at various points if the dog remains in proper position for extended lengths of time. As soon as you come to a halt, the dog is to sit. At first you will need to issue the sit command, but as the dog becomes adept at heeling, the sit will become automatic when you stop and no verbal cue will be needed.

As willing to learn as your Labrador may be, mastering the heel will take time. As you encounter problems—usually surging ahead—you may want to resort to placing the dog in a sit to restore calm rather than continually snapping it back into position. Having the dog sit will allow it to succeed at a task it is already familiar with, and thereby receive praise. This will keep everyone at ease and help the heeling practice continue rather than break down into confusion on the dog's part and anger on the trainer's. Once the dog has successfully completed the

sit, move him out with "Jake, heel!" Praise him if he comes and moves in the proper position. Stop him as soon as he misbehaves, giving a firm tug on the lead and a stern look. It is imperative that you do not apply continuous pressure from the lead on the neck of the surging dog, as this will mean that the choke is continually applied.

The choke is meant to be a sudden jarring that regains the dog's attention and brings about a correction. It must be swift and strong enough to get a response, but not so strong as to cause pain and possible injury.

Remember: The choke should be used only when needed, should have impact on the dog, and should be immediately released.

During the early stages of training, keep the lessons short, no more than 10 to 15 minutes. As the dog becomes more adept—and no longer needs to be put into frequent corrective sits—extend the lessons as energy and interest permit.

Stay

The "stay" command builds from the sit. Do not attempt to teach the stay until the dog is reliably performing the sit, as the dog will be required to remain in this position until released. Begin by placing it in a sit. Keep some slight upward pressure on its neck from the lead in your right hand. As you command "Stay!" you must simultaneously move away from the dog, using your right leg, and bring the palm of your left hand down toward its face, stopping short of touching its muzzle. Move only a short distance (about a foot at first). Make sure that the hand signal is given at the same time that the command is given and the step is taken. Retain eye contact, if possible. Repeat the command while maintaining the signal. The voice should be firm and authoritative. Do not expect the dog to stay for more than ten seconds or so at first, so release after a small success.

When the dog breaks the stay, return it immediately to sit and repeat the whole procedure. It is normal for the dog to try to move toward you once it sees you move away, or to lie down once it sees that it is to remain where positioned. Be patient and do not expect immediate results. Your Labrador retriever is brainy and will catch on fairly quickly, but do not push it by endless repetitions. As you see improvement, you will extend the length of time for the stay and the distance moved, with a desired end result being a dog that can be relied upon to stay in the sit position for at least several minutes. (The down-stay, to be taught later, can and should be used daily as a control method that has the dog lying down for 30 minutes or more as a means of teaching the importance of discipline and enforcing your position as leader.)

Come

The "come" is a basic command that is quite easy to teach, as Labrador retrievers instinctively respond to the sound of their master's voice and will all but stop in their tracks to focus on the sound. The come teaches a dog that it must return to its master at once, without hesitation. It is a command that will enforce the owner's leadership position, as the dog will stop whatever it is doing and return on command to its master's side. The come command can also be a life-saving tool used to remove the dog immediately from a dangerous situation.

Most likely you have given your Lab informal training in this command from the beginning of your relationship with the dog, as even pups will happily come when called in anticipation of play, food, or various pleasant exchanges. The goal is to have the dog respond to your call regardless of the circumstances or how it perceives the situation (thereby overcoming the "What's in it for me?" syndrome).

Formal training for the come command should begin with a pleasant play period. Place the dog on a long lead (20 feet [6.1 m] or more) and let it romp in the practice yard, maintaining only minimal tension at the end of the lead. Once the dog is relaxed and concentrating on play or investigation of some nearby object, command "Jake, come!" in a firm tone and snap the lead to start the dog in motion to you. Praise as the dog *begins* to move toward you, and have him come directly to you and into a sit. Should he fail to respond, give a sharp correction with the lead as you repeat "Jake, come!" If necessary, repeat the command and reel the dog in by slowly retracting the cord, but this is rarely required. Once the dog has completed the come and the companion command of sit, release with "Good boy!" and let him move away from you. Repeat the come command at various intervals, and enforce with a sharp tug on the lead should the dog fail to move immediately toward you.

When teaching the "stay," be sure to place the palm down and swing the hand toward the dog as you give the command .

Use of the come should not be overdone. Perform a few repetitions during all training lessons, and at various points throughout the day when the dog's presence really is requested. *Never* command a dog to come and then punish it for an offense once it arrives at your side. If you catch your dog in an inappropriate action, *go to it* and reprimand. Should you call the dog with "Come!" and then proceed to punish it when it arrives, you will almost certainly ruin your chances of having a dog that will instantly return to you when called, thus negating this command's importance and reliability.

Down

The "down" command is tied closely to the sit and stay commands. To teach the dog to lie down, place it first in a sit and kneel next to it. As you command "Down!" take hold of its front legs near the body, gently lift them from the floor, and lower the dog to the ground. Once down, command the dog to "Down, stay!" Follow this with "Good boy" if it remains in the prone position. You may need to keep your left hand resting on its back to keep it from getting up. Pet briefly, release by motioning upward with your hand and gently tugging the lead, and return the dog to a sit, on command, to begin again.

Do not make your dog remain in the down position too long at first, as the down concept needs to be reinforced to keep it clearly differentiated from the stay. Be sure the dog remains lying on all fours for the short downs, not sprawled out. The dog is to be alert on the down, not overly comfortable.

Practice the down several times each day. As the downward movement becomes more familiar, you will soon be able to stop guiding the legs down and return to a standing position. During this transition you may want to issue the command and try just slapping the floor with the palm of your hand to get the dog moving down. Alternatively, you can place the lead under your left foot, keeping the lead rather taut. As you command "Down!" a slight pressure on the dog's shoulders should be sufficient to give it the idea. Your Labrador will probably be lying down at your side with only a verbal command within a few days.

As your dog progresses, you can teach it to lie down on lead from various positions, such as in front of you, from a distance, etc. You may want to incorporate a down motion with your hand in time with the down command to augment these exercises. When practicing indoors, you should occasionally have the dog work off leash, but do not accept sloppy performance, as many dogs tend to be less businesslike once the lead is removed. The dog should never be allowed off leash in an unconfined outdoor area until it has proven itself truly trustworthy (that is, shown a mastery of all the basic commands). And even then, an exciting scent may lure away even a well-trained and disciplined Labrador—so always use caution when the dog is off leash.

The down is a valuable lesson for all concerned. As owner, you should train the dog to perform an extended down-stay *daily*. With practice, you will soon be able to have your dog remain in a downstay for 30 minutes or more. This is a vital aspect of training a house pet, as it will reinforce your position as leader in the dog's mind and will give you the control you need at times to remove the dog from any activities you do not care for it to participate in (such as hanging around the dinner table while you are eating, creating a scene when company comes, etc.) without having to lock the dog up somewhere. This is not punishment. A properly trained dog can be placed in an extended down-stay near its owner, yet in a place where it can relax too, such as across the room or in a corner.

Begin with stays of a few minutes and then gradually increase the time, but do it irregularly—8 minutes, then 5 minutes the next time, 15 minutes the next. In this way the dog will not anticipate when it will be finished and will truly learn to obey the command. Should the dog become bored and start to break the stay, tell it "No, stay!" and replace it. *You* must determine when the dog may rejoin you. As the dog becomes accustomed to the long down, it will oftentimes fall asleep. This is perfectly acceptable as long as it remains where it was placed when it awakens. You should, however, wake the dog with a tap of the foot near the head when it is time for the release (try not to startle it). Do not let it sleep on indefinitely, as you need to formally complete the exercise. Always end the long down-stay with the upward release motion and praise.

The down can also be an effective lifesaving command to immediately stop a dog from participating in or entering into a dangerous situation. Once you are certain that the dog understands the down concept, the down can be practiced while walking, not just from the sit. Teaching a dog to drop down on command while in motion takes time, but is well worth the

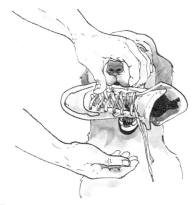

To get your Labrador to release an object from its mouth, apply slight pressure at the back of the muzzle and command the dog to "drop" or "give."

effort. For example. your well-trained Labrador has been let out for a brisk romp in the backyard and has wandered too far, across the road. Labradors are wanderers by nature, easily distracted by a new scent or sight. Upon seeing you, it immediately begins to run toward you—and into oncoming traffic. You command "Down!" and the dog immediately drops to the ground. Such a case is the extreme, but it emphasizes the importance of the down command and the fact that only an immediate response to the command is acceptable.

When training your dog to retrieve, give equal importance to teaching it to release the object. Many dogs will want to play tug-of-war or tease about releasing when they return. To make your dog a reliable retriever, enforce the "drop" or "give" command every time a retrieve is made.

If the dog balks, place it in a sit and remove the object. Do not allow the dog to run away. Once a proper return has been completed, praise the dog and either throw again or end the session with lots of praise.

Training Problems

There is no foolproof method for training all dogs, as problems often arise that interfere with the learning process. Finding the solution to such problems is generally a matter of trial and error and perseverance. The place to start is to evaluate your teaching technique.

• Are your commands clear, concise, and consistent?

• Are you giving the dog ample time to learn, not rushing it?

• Do you speak in a firm, authoritative tone (never shouting, scolding or whining)?

• Do you praise the dog enough to make learning a pleasant experience?

• Are you concentrating? If you feel the problem is with the student and not the teacher, observe the dog's behavior and body language.

• Is the dog easily distracted? You may be training in an area that presents too many distractions for a beginner. Try a more secluded training site and see if concentration improves.

• Is this lapse a new occurrence or constant? A sudden disinterest or confusion in a male can be caused by a local bitch in heat. Alternatively, the dog may have reached a temporary learning plateau (common during the fifth or sixth week of training) and appear to have forgotten all it has learned. This odd phenomenon is not unusual and generally passes in a week's time.

• Is the dog ill? Many maladies are hard to spot. A dog that is reluctant to move freely or jump may be showing the early signs of hip dysplasia. Eliminate the health issue with a thorough examination by a veterinarian.

If, despite your best efforts, disorder still prevails in your training program, consult a professional trainer (preferably one with a knowledge of Labradors). An expert eye can often quickly spot the underlying fault and propose corrective measures. Sometimes all that is needed is a new approach or technique that the dog will like better. Sometimes a lesson in discipline is called for. Never let training setbacks (and there *will* be some) escalate to the extremes— where you lash out at the dog or give up in despair. Help from a more experienced trainer, and dedication to the task, should get your Labrador back to work.

Breeding Quality Labradors

Producing a Best-in-Show winning Labrador or a titlist is the dream of most established breeders and many have garnered such distinctions. Few, however, arrive at such an end product without extensive knowledge of the pedigree behind their dogs and the experience that aids in a good selection of sire and dam.

If I may be so bold, I want to state once again at the beginning of this chapter on breeding that I personally feel that only dogs of superior quality should be bred. (I am sure this prejudice has already been made clear.) Each new generation should be equal to or better than the one that preceded

Considerations Before Breeding

The demand for Labrador retrievers is increasing as the breed's popularity spreads. While it is possible to breed quality Labradors and make a profit, this should not be a primary motive.

To produce good dogs costs a considerable amount of money, especially in the first few litters. (Consider the initial purchase of quality breeding stock, stud service, as well as the feeding and health care of an average litter of ten puppies.) Also consider the amount of time and energy required. Raising puppies is hard work. The older they get, the more they eat, the dirtier they get, and the more you must do to keep them protected.

it—and this requires informed, planned matings. Every Labrador retriever should not only be physically pleasing, but also endowed with the original breed characteristics and able to perform the original tasks. With too many random matings some of this ancestry is bound to be lost, as faults are spread rather than eliminated.

Selection of a Sire and a Dam

Every dog is the product of the genes passed to it by its ancestors—and these genes stem from generations back. Quality genes consistently passed through the generations are what breeders look and hope for, and novice breeders should bear this in mind when taking on this role. Many beginners interested in breeding for competition err by breeding titlist to titlist assuming that quality to quality will produce quality. It may, or it may not. While sire and dam may each be of superior conformation, each may carry differing traits that do not complement the partner's, and the resulting puppies may well be of lesser conformation quality than the parents.

The brood bitch is the heart of a breeding program, so care must be taken in her selection. Because of this, many breeders will be reluctant to part with a promising female puppy. Many novice breeders opt to obtain a proven quality-producing bitch from an established kennel (again, if the breeder will part with one), as this will eliminate some of the uncertainty of breeding a maiden dam. However, such a dog is often quite expensive.

Evaluate each candidate carefully, keeping the standard and your breeding goal in mind. Aim for a dog of superior quality, allowing one major fault that can be bred out in a generation or two by selective breeding. If you start with less, you will be fighting an uphill battle to produce quality. There are, however, instances where bitches that are mediocre in appearance produce high-quality offspring regardless of which dog they are bred to. Such dogs are sound and typical in conformation and *always* well bred. Their offspring reflect the quality of their ancestors, so do not necessarily cast off a potential dam that the breeder feels may produce better than herself.

In selecting a stud dog, a breeder has many options. The emphasis is on finding a stud that will enhance and complement the qualities of the hitch. An experienced stud that has already produced quality offspring is, of course, preferable. Whether a breeder plans to linebreed, inbreed, or outcross (see page 86), a good Labrador retriever stud should be of correct size, well-balanced, with good coat and pigmentation, a good mover, and as free of obvious faults as possible.

If you know an experienced breeder, seek his or her advice whenever possible. A breeder not involved with either your Labrador or its potential mate will probably be more objective in evaluating their quality. Such a breeder will be most effective in helping evaluate the litter produced and in guiding the future course of your breeding program.

When considering a mating, begin by studying the potential sire and dam's pedigrees. A pedigree was probably supplied at the time you purchased your dog, if you bought from an established breeder whom you informed of your possible intent to breed. If you did not receive one, ask the breeder to try to reconstruct this information, because a pedigree is more than just a list of names. A pedigree can indicate what type of breeding system your dog stems from.

Most breeders will prepare a three-generation pedigree which lists information back to the great-grandsires and great-granddams of your puppy. Extensive four- and five-generation pedigrees will disclose information on another 16 and 32 ancestors respectively, but few people need these details as there is believed to be little genetic effect from ancestors beyond three generations. You should, however, trace the past histories as far as possible for any incidents of hip dysplasia, epilepsy, progressive retinal atrophy, and retinal dysplasia, which are hereditary diseases. Any dogs carrying these diseases should be eliminated from all breeding programs.

Breeding Systems

There are three types of breeding systems: linebreeding, inbreeding, and outcrossing. These systems all aim at strengthening desirable traits and eliminating faults through selective breeding, but they go about it in different ways.

Linebreeding

Linebreeding is a process of mating related dogs that are removed from each other by at least one generation (cousins, grandson to granddaughter, grandmother to grandson, etc.). The breeding pair shares a common quality ancestor (usually in the second or third generation) that is known to pass on its desirable traits to its progeny. Linebreeding enables a breeder to set or "fix" correct type in his or her stock by breeding quality genes in successive generations. This method limits the flow of new genes into a breeding stock. The emphasis is on eliminating faults by establishing prepotency of desired traits.

These charming puppies show two of the allowable colors for Labrador retrievers—yellow and black. The black coloring should be all black; a small white spot on the chest is permissible (although not desirable). Yellows can range from fox-red to light cream, with variations in shading on the ears, back, and underparts.

Inbreeding

Inbreeding is the mating of closely related dogs, with typical pairings being daughter to father, son to mother, sister to brother. Such close matings intensify the genes present in the bloodline. Such breedings are not recommended.

Outcrossing

Outcrossing is a system that attempts to eliminate faults by pairing partners which may complement each other. The dogs to be mated do not share ancestors in the first five generations, but each is prepotent in traits that the partner is lacking. This is not random selection. For example, a brood bitch from a line known for good hindquarters but faulty fronts would be mated with a stud dog with a strong family line of good fronts. Outcrossing is generally resorted to when linebreeding fails to bring about a correction for a particular fault and a line that is felt to be complementary is used to compensate. There are no guarantees of a "simple" correction, however. This adds new genes to the bloodline, rather than intensifying genes that already exist.

The haphazard mating of totally unrelated Labradors is termed *outbreeding*. This is the usual pattern for the mating of neighborhood pets. If this pattern is continued for generations, a degeneration in quality and breed character is likely to occur as the genes become a vast assortment of possibilities. First generation outbred puppies will generally be quite hardy and robust, exhibiting what is known as *hybrid vigor*. With each successive outbred generation the faults become more apparent and permanently entrenched.

Color inheritance in the Labrador retriever follows a genetic pattern. Black is the dominant color, but coats of yellow or chocolate can appear if recessive genes for these colors are present in both parents.

Coat Color Inheritance

There are three acceptable coat colors in the Labrador retriever: black, yellow (with variation from fox-red to light cream), and chocolate. Black is the most common color, but the numbers of yellows and chocolates are on the rise.

Coat color is determined by the type of genes received from each of the parents. Black is the dominant color genetically. Simply put, if there is a black gene present in the dog's makeup, the dog will be black. A yellow coat is produced when a dog receives a recessive gene for this color from both of its parents. In the absence of a dominant black gene, the recessive genes can be expressed. Because of this, a black dog can produce yellow or chocolate offspring if it carries both a dominant black gene and a hidden recessive.

The chocolate color is also a recessive, but many variables come into play regarding the inheritance pattern of this color. The recessive chocolate factor can be carried by both black and yellow Labradors. There may also be a crossover or modifying effect involved with the chocolate recessive, because in several generations of breeding chocolate to chocolate a breakdown in pigmentation, eye coloring, and overall coat color often occurs. It is common practice for breeders of the chocolates to breed back to a black every so often to keep this fading problem in check and upgrade quality.

Building a Breeding Program

It is best to wait to breed your Labrador retriever bitch until she has reached maturity and had at least two heats or "seasons." Generally, 18 to 24 months of age is regarded as the best age for a Labrador's first mating, as she will be physically and mentally able to withstand the rigors of whelping and raising a litter of puppies. This is a time of peak physical conditioning, and may conflict with the timing of a show career. In most cases, having and nursing a litter will have negligible after-effects and may, in fact, add a suppleness often lacking in young females.

A healthy, quality-producing Labrador can be bred every other season until approximately six or seven years of age, if all previous litters have been uncomplicated. If, for some reason, she is bred two seasons in a row, she will need at least a year of rest to recuperate and regain her strength and stamina.

State of Health

It is essential that the bitch and stud both be in good physical condition at the time of the mating. The bitch should have been given a prebreeding examination by her veterinarian approximately one month before mating to determine her state of health and if any vaccinations or controls for internal or external parasites are needed. Both dogs should be certified free of hip dysplasia and eye disorders.

Mating

A female will be ready for mating on approximately the tenth day after the onset of the heat cycle. In the early days of the cycle, she is attractive to males but will not allow coitus. Ovulation generally occurs around the ninth day into the cycle, after which time the bitch is fertile. With most arranged stud services, the female is usually taken to the stud dog, as females generally adapt more quickly to a new environment and are not put off by strange surroundings. To insure a successful fertilization, she is often bred twice, with a day's interval between matings.

Plan on having two handlers present during the mating to help control and soothe the animals. The handlers should speak in soft tones and help position the dogs if either partner is inexperienced. The stud dog will mount the female from the rear and grasp her middle with his front legs. Once the dog has penetrated the female and ejaculation has taken place, a section of his penis will swell and the two dogs will be "tied" together for a period of up to 30 minutes. The handlers should remain and supervise until the tie is naturally broken. Any attempt to force a break can cause serious damage—both physical and emotional—to both stud and bitch, so attention must be paid to keeping both dogs calm during this time.

Pregnancy

Gestation for puppies is approximately 63 days. During the first few weeks the bitch may have some slight increase in appetite and some swelling of the breasts. The pregnancy can usually be confirmed by palpation by a veterinarian at 28 days after mating *(never do this yourself!)*.

During the pregnancy, the bitch should be fed the same well-balanced diet that she is used to. No supplementation is usually needed in the first four or five weeks. During the last weeks she will need additional calories (primarily in the form of protein) to compensate for the requirements of the rapidly growing puppies. An increase of 30 to 50 percent can be expected by whelping time. Her meals should be given in small doses three or four times a day to help avoid the discomfort a large meal may cause her.

A dog in whelp should be allowed to go about her day in her usual way. It is very important for her to continue exercising, as this will maintain muscle tone and aid in the delivery. Vigorous exercise should be eliminated during the last two to three weeks, as well as jumping and climbing stairs. As delivery approaches, she will slow down her activities and seek out her "nest." You should introduce her to the whelping area before delivery is imminent and allow her to adjust to it. If not, she may seek out her own, less suitable spot (such as your linen closet).

During the weeks prior to delivery, stock up on the following supplies and place them on a table by the whelping box: washcloths, blunt-tipped scissors, a heating pad (to keep the puppies warm), waxed dental floss (for cords), a scale, paper towels, a wastebasket, and a cloth-lined box to place newborns in while others are being born.

You will need to prepare (or buy) a whelping box in which the dam will have the litter and raise them for the first few weeks. The box should be low enough to allow the dam to come and go easily, yet high enough to keep the puppies in for several weeks. It should be large enough to allow the bitch to lie on her side and stretch out, but not overly large so that puppies can crawl too far away from the warmth of the mother. Many breeders build a "guard" rail several inches in width, placed several inches up the sides, to serve as a barrier that prevents the mother from inadvertently crushing the newborns against the side walls. The bottom should initially be lined with layers of newspaper, which can be easily removed for the frequent required cleanings. Place the box in a warm, dry, draft-free location that is out of normal family traffic.

Delivery

Approximately 24 hours before delivery the bitch's temperature will fall to 99°F (37.2°C) or lower. Encourage her to rest. As delivery draws near, she will appear agitated and begin to pant heavily. She may vomit. The abdomen will begin its contractions. A first-time mother may be anxious at this point (not to mention

first-time breeders!). Speak to her constantly in soft, soothing tones. Encourage her.

Labrador retrievers seldom run into problems during the birth of puppies, but you should notify your veterinarian to be on the ready as whelping time nears. Inexperienced breeders should ask a more knowledgeable breeder to assist them.

Each puppy will arrive enclosed in a membrane sac, which must be removed in a matter of minutes to allow the newborn to begin breathing on its own. Should the dog fail to tear the sac open and cut the umbilical cord, be prepared to step in quickly and perform this task (get a briefing from your veterinarian on this procedure prior to delivery). The placenta should be expelled within several minutes of each birth. Check that you see one placenta for each whelp, as none should be retained. Do not be surprised if the bitch eats a few of the placentas. This is normal and not harmful.

The average Labrador litter is eight to ten, but a litter of 17 has been reported. Allow the dam to lick and

This Labrador dam is nursing her pups in a well-designed whelping box that allows adequate space and comfort. It contains a safety railing that prevents the dam from accidentally rolling on and crushing a puppy that is lodged along the side.

During the first days after birth, the puppies will sleep most of the time. In a few weeks, however, their energy level will increase greatly.

suckle each newborn, but remove them when the birth of the next whelp is in progress. At this time you can gently wipe the puppy clean, weigh it, and temporarily place it in the heated holding box until all deliveries are over.

A typical Labrador retriever dam will take naturally to motherhood and exhibit a gentle touch with her puppies and a tolerance for human onlookers. Praise her lavishly and often for a job well done.

Caution: Dams that show any disinterest or aversion to the puppies should be carefully watched to prevent any possible harm coming to the litter. Such dams should be removed from future breeding plans.

Newborn Puppies

A newborn whelp must be kept in a warm environment—approximately 85°F (29.4°C)—for its first two weeks of life. This is essential to its well-being. The dam will attend to all the puppies' basic needs, including stimulating them to urinate and defecate and cleaning up after them. A breeder should carefully tend to the dam's needs the first few days and keep the whelping area very clean. Each puppy should be picked up and handled on a regular basis. Check it for overall health and monitor its weight gain.

The puppies should be shown lots of affection from the earliest days to start the bonding process. Newborns can be gently stroked, caressed, and softly spoken to from birth, as such stimulation is known to heighten their awareness and ability to interact with man. The puppies' eyes and ears will begin to open at about 10 days, and stimulations such as soft music and visual backgrounds encourage prompt development of the senses.

Many breeders of hunting dogs feel that the puppies should be exposed to loud noises and vigorous (though not dangerous) handling from birth. It is believed that by early indoctrination into stressful situations, puppies destined for the hunt will turn into adults that are steadfast and not easily frightened by the sounds of gunfire.

The weaning process can begin at approximately three weeks of age. This begins the transition to adulthood, and the puppy will be required to master canine and human socialization in just a few week's time—as well as learning how to run, cavort, and carry on like a thrill-seeking puppy. Breeders should take time to handle each puppy as much as possible, giving each a daily grooming with a soft brush and a physical inspection. This grooming will require the wriggling puppy to submit to its human master—its first introduction to the human "alpha" figure.

These healthy pups nurse contentedly from their dam.

Puppies cling together for warmth and security.

These puppies will soon outgrow the walls of their whelping box.

Puppies learn quickly how to drink from a bowl and will soon switch to solid food.

Useful Addresses and Literature

Retriever Clubs

Labrador Retriever Club of America*
  Christopher G. Winck
  9690 Wilson Mills Road
  Chardon, OH 44024

National Amateur Retriever Club
  Dorothy A. Metcalf
  Route 1, Box 92
  Oxford, MD 21654

National Retriever Club
  Oscar S. Brewer
  27th Floor, Commerce Tower
  P.O. Box 13367
  Kansas City, MO 64199

These addresses may change as new officers are elected. The latest listing can always be obtained from the American Kennel Club.

Kennel Clubs

For general information:
  American Kennel Club
  51 Madison Avenue
  New York, NY 10038
  212-696-8200

For registration, records, or litter information:
  5580 Centerview Drive
  Raleigh, NC 27606

Australian National Kennel Club
  Royal Show Grounds
  Ascot Vale
  Victoria
  Australia

Canadian Kennel Club
  111 Eglington Avenue
  Toronto 12, Ontario
  Canada

Irish Kennel Club
  41 Harcourt Street
  Dublin 2
  Ireland

The Kennel Club
  1-4 Clargis Street
  Picadilly
  London, W7Y 8AB
  England

New Zealand Kennel Club
  P.O. Box 523
  Wellington
  New Zealand

Publications

American Field
  American Field Publishing Company
  222 West Adams Street
  Chicago, IL 60606
  (Journal dating from 1874; covers all sporting breeds.)

Hunter's Whistle, The
  American Kennel Club
  51 Madison Avenue
  New York, NY 10038
  (Bi-monthly newsletter; provides information on upcoming field trial and hunting tests.)

Retriever Field Trial News
  4213 South Howell Avenue
  Milwaukee, WI 53207

(Joint publication of the National Amateur Retriever Club and the National Retriever Club; compiles field trial statistics and covers news of the sport in the United States and Canada.)

Books

Alderton, David, *The Dog Care Manual,* Barron's Educational Series, Inc., Hauppauge, New York, 1986.

Barish, Eileen, *Vacationing with Your Pet!,* Pet-Friendly Publications, Scottsdale, Arizona, 1994.

Baer, Ted, *Communicating with Your Dog,* Barron's Educational Series, Inc. Hauppauge, New York, 1989.

Carlson, Delbert G., D.V.M., and Griffin, James M., M.D., *Dog Owner's Home Veterinary Handbook,* Howell Book House, New York, 1980.

Fogle, Bruce, D.V.M., M.R.C.V.S., *The Dog's Mind: Understanding Your Dog's Behavior,* Howell Book House, New York, 1990.

Frye, Fredric, *First Aid for Your Dog,* Barron's Educational Series, Inc., Hauppauge, New York, 1987.

Klever, Ulrich, *The Complete Book of Dog Care,* Barron's Educational Series, Inc., Hauppauge, New York, 1989.

Pinney, Chris C., *Guide to Home Pet Grooming,* Barron's Educational Series, Inc., Hauppauge, New York, 1990.

Wrede, Barbara, *Civilizing Your Puppy,* Barron's Educational Series, Inc., Hauppauge, New York, 1992.

Index

BARRON'S PET REFERENCE BOOKS

Barron's Pet Reference Books are and have long been the choice of experts and discerning pet owners. Why? Here are just a few reasons. These indispensable volumes are packed with 35 to 200 stunning full-color photos. Each provides the very latest expert information and answers questions that pet owners often wonder about.

BARRON'S PET REFERENCE BOOKS ARE:

AQUARIUM FISH (1350-6)
AQUARIUM FISH BREEDING (4474-6)
THE AQUARIUM FISH SURVIVAL MANUAL
  (5686-8)
BEFORE YOU BUY THAT PUPPY (1750-1)
THE BEST PET NAME BOOK EVER (4258-1)
CARING FOR YOUR SICK CAT (1726-9)
THE COMPLETE BOOK OF BUDGERIGARS
  (6059-8)
THE CAT CARE MANUAL (5765-1)
CIVILIZING YOUR PUPPY (4953-5)
COMMUNICATING WITH YOUR DOG (4203-4)
THE COMPLETE BOOK OF CAT CARE (4613-7)
THE COMPLETE BOOK OF DOG CARE (4158-5)
THE DOG CARE MANUAL (5764-3)

FIRST AID FOR YOUR CAT (5827-5)
FIRST AID FOR YOUR DOG (5828-3)
GOLDFISH AND ORNAMENTAL CARP (5634-5)
GUIDE TO HOME PET GROOMING (4298-0)
HEALTHY DOG, HAPPY DOG (1842-7)
HOP TO IT: A Guide to Training Your Pet Rabbit
  (4551-3)
THE HORSE CARE MANUAL (5795-3)
HOW TO TEACH YOUR OLD DOG NEW TRICKS
  (4544-0)
LABYRINTH FISH (5635-3)
THE COMPLETE BOOK OF MACAWS (6073-3)
NONVENOMOUS SNAKES (5632-9)
THE COMPLETE BOOK OF PARROTS (5971-9)
WATER PLANTS IN THE AQUARIUM (3926-2)

Barron's Educational Series, Inc., 250 Wireless Boulevard, Hauppauge, New York 11788. For faster service call toll-free: 1-800-645-3476.

In Canada: Georgetown Book Warehouse, 34 Armstrong Avenue, Georgetown, Ontario L7G 4R9. Call toll-free: 1-800-247-7160.

Books can be purchased at your bookstore or directly from Barron's. Enclose check or money order for total amount plus sales tax where applicable and 10% for postage (minimum charge $3.75. Can. $4.00). All major credit cards are accepted. Prices subject to change without notice. ISBN Prefix: 0-8120   R 8/94

Perfect for Pet Owners!

PET OWNER'S MANUALS

Over 50 illustrations per book (20 or more color photos), 72–80 pp., paperback.

AFRICAN GRAY PARROTS (3773-1)
AMAZON PARROTS (4035-X)
BANTAMS (3687-5)
BEAGLES (3829-0)
BEEKEEPING (4089-9)
BOSTON TERRIERS (1696-3)
BOXERS (4036-8)
CANARIES (4611-0)
CATS (4442-8)
CHINCHILLAS (4037-6)
CHOW-CHOWS (3952-1)
CICHLIDS (4597-1)
COCKATIELS (4610-2)
COCKER SPANIELS (1478-2)
COCKATOOS (4159-3)
COLLIES (1875-3)
CONURES (4880-6)
DACHSHUNDS (1843-5)
DALMATIANS (4605-6)
DISCUS FISH (4669-2)
DOBERMAN PINSCHERS (2999-2)
DOGS (4822-9)
DOVES (1855-9)
DWARF RABBITS (1352-2)
ENGLISH SPRINGER SPANIELS (1778-1)
FEEDING AND SHELTERING BACKYARD
   BIRDS (4252-2)
FEEDING AND SHELTERING EUROPEAN
   BIRDS (2858-9)
FERRETS (2976-3)
GERBILS (3725-1)
GERMAN SHEPHERDS (2982-8)
GOLDEN RETRIEVERS (3793-6)
GOLDFISH (2975-5)
GOULDIAN FINCHES (4523-8)
GREAT DANES (1418-9)
GUINEA PIGS (4612-9)
GUPPIES, MOLLIES, AND PLATTIES (1497-9)
HAMSTERS (4439-8)
IRISH SETTERS (4663-3)
KEESHONDEN (1560-6)
KILLIFISH (4475-4)
LABRADOR RETRIEVERS (3792-8)
LHASA APSOS (3950-5)
LIZARDS IN THE TERRARIUM (3925-4)
LONGHAIRED CATS (2803-1)
LONG-TAILED PARAKEETS (1351-4)

LORIES AND LORIKEETS (1567-3)
LOVEBIRDS (3726-X)
MACAWS (4768-0)
MICE (2921-6)
MUTTS (4126-7)
MYNAHS (3688-3)
PARAKEETS (4437-1)
PARROTS (4823-7)
PERSIAN CATS (4405-3)
PIGEONS (4044-9)
POMERANIANS (4670-6)
PONIES (2856-2)
POODLES (2812-0)
POT BELLIES AND OTHER MINIATURE PIGS
   (1356-5)
PUGS (1824-9)
RABBITS (4440-1)
RATS (4535-1)
ROTTWEILERS (4483-5)
SCHNAUZERS (3949-1)
SCOTTISH FOLD CATS (4999-3)
SHAR-PEI (4334-2)
SHEEP (4091-0)
SHETLAND SHEEPDOGS (4264-6)
SHIH TZUS (4524-6)
SIAMESE CATS (4764-8)
SIBERIAN HUSKIES (4265-4)
SMALL DOGS (1951-2)
SNAKES (2813-9)
SPANIELS (2424-9)
TROPICAL FISH (4700-1)
TURTLES (4702-8)
WEST HIGHLAND WHITE TERRIERS (1950-4)
YORKSHIRE TERRIERS (4406-1)
ZEBRA FINCHES (3497-X)

NEW PET HANDBOOKS

Detailed, illustrated profiles (40–60 color photos), 144 pp., paperback.

NEW AQUARIUM FISH HANDBOOK (3682-4)
NEW AUSTRALIAN PARAKEET
   HANDBOOK (4739-7)
NEW BIRD HANDBOOK (4157-7)
NEW CANARY HANDBOOK (4879-2)
NEW CAT HANDBOOK (2922-4)
NEW COCKATIEL HANDBOOK (4201-8)
NEW DOG HANDBOOK (2857-0)
NEW DUCK HANDBOOK (4088-0)
NEW FINCH HANDBOOK (2859-7)
NEW GOAT HANDBOOK (4090-2)

NEW PARAKEET HANDBOOK (2985-2)
NEW PARROT HANDBOOK (3729-4)
NEW RABBIT HANDBOOK (4202-6)
NEW SALTWATER AQUARIUM
   HANDBOOK (4482-7)
NEW SOFTBILL HANDBOOK (4075-9)
NEW TERRIER HANDBOOK (3951-3)

REFERENCE BOOKS

Comprehensive, lavishly illustrated references (60–300 color photos), 136–176 pp., hardcover & paperback.

AQUARIUM FISH (1350-6)
AQUARIUM FISH BREEDING (4474-6)
AQUARIUM FISH SURVIVAL MANUAL
   (5686-8)
AQUARIUM PLANTS MANUAL (1687-4)
BEFORE YOU BUY THAT PUPPY (1750-1)
BEST PET NAME BOOK EVER, THE
   (4258-1)
CARING FOR YOUR SICK CAT (1726-9)
CAT CARE MANUAL (5765-1)
CIVILIZING YOUR PUPPY (4953-5)
COMMUNICATING WITH YOUR DOG
   (4203-4)
COMPLETE BOOK OF BUDGERIGARS
   (6059-8)
COMPLETE BOOK OF CAT CARE (4613-7)
COMPLETE BOOK OF DOG CARE (4158-5)
COMPLETE BOOK OF PARROTS (5971-9)
DOG CARE MANUAL (5764-3)
FEEDING YOUR PET BIRD (1521-3)
GOLDFISH AND ORNAMENTAL CARP
   (9286-4)
GUIDE TO A WELL BEHAVED CAT
   (1476-6)
GUIDE TO HOME PET GROOMING
   (4298-0)
HEALTHY DOG, HAPPY DOG (1842-7)
HOP TO IT: A Guide to Training Your Pet Rabbit
   (4551-3)
HORSE CARE MANUAL (1133-3)
HOW TO TALK TO YOUR CAT (1749-8)
HOW TO TEACH YOUR OLD DOG
   NEW TRICKS (4544-0)
LABYRINTH FISH (5635-3)
MACAWS (9037-3)
NONVENOMOUS SNAKES (5632-9)
WATER PLANTS IN THE AQUARIUM (3926-2)

Barron's Educational Series, Inc. • 250 Wireless Blvd., Hauppauge, NY 11788
Call toll-free: 1-800-645-3476 • In Canada: Georgetown Book Warehouse
34 Armstrong Ave., Georgetown, Ont. L7G 4R9 • Call toll-free: 1-800-247-7160
ISBN prefix: 0-8120 • Order from your favorite book or pet store

R 6/94